Dementia's Unexpected Gifts

A memoir of stumbling into caregiving, then learning to live my best life

BARBARA F. LUEBKE

A Red Fish Book

ISBN: 979-8-6891476-8-0

Printed in the United States of America

For Caregivers

*"Even when you don't notice it,
life is rearranging you."*

The character Ellie in
The Daughters of Eerietown
Connie Schulz

*"You do not need to know precisely what is
happening, or exactly where it is all going. What
you need is to recognize the possibilities and
challenges offered by the present moment, and to
embrace them with courage, faith and hope."*

Thomas Merton

Contents

"Senility is best described in the old tongue, duine le Dia, for in that phrase is a kinder, more understanding view of the condition. Its literal meaning is 'a person of God,' for only the person's maker now can understand him."

John Connell
The Farmer's Son

Author's Note

It is important to me that I begin by acknowledging the "privileges" that have had an impact on the journey I describe.

- Family support

- Financial security and independence

- Education

But as became obvious to me (painfully at times), there also are "disadvantages" that at times have made my journey more difficult.

- A too-small circle of friends

- A tendency to be overly cerebral

- An aversion to "group talk"

I hope neither these advantages nor disadvantages alienate me from caregivers in other circumstances. We have much to learn from one another.

As I contemplated writing a book, I grappled with the issue of privacy. More than most, my "well" partner was hypersensitive about keeping the personal private. Dementia wears away at privacy, however, and modesty eventually rests with the behaviors of others. How can I tell an honest story while showing respect for my partner's essential self? I decided the following:

- I will refer to my partner as ME. (Yes, those who know me will know of whom I write. But most in that small universe already know at least parts of this story.) I also will use initials for people where it feels appropriate to me. For all others, I will use first names only.

- I will respect our 30-year relationship. I know ME would insist that I be circumspect about certain details, and I will do my best to honor that and the love we share.

- I am fortunate to have years of emails sent and received, photographs, detailed notes totaling thousands of words that I wrote along the way, and a reporter's knack for recalling events and conversations. I will draw on all of those to write accurately and truthfully.

- As much as possible, I will avoid describing specific indignities of ME's dementia and particular behaviors that would only cause embarrassment. In no way do I mean to sugarcoat the realities of the disease, but caregivers know them or sooner or later will.

- By the same token, I will not shy away from discussing my own frustrations with and responses to such behaviors. I am telling *my* story, and I will strive to be honest, transparent and as complete as possible in sharing my thoughts, feelings and actions.

Late into this journey, I came across the term "neurocognitive impairments" in an advertisement. That got me thinking about "diagnosis" and related terms, in particular dementia and Alzheimer's. I concluded that for us ordinary folks, it doesn't matter which term is used. The outcome is the same. So I use the terms interchangeably.

Finally, a word about the quotations preceding each chapter. Just as interest in a particular model car causes us to notice them more frequently, so I found my reading self being drawn to passages that spoke to me about life as I was experiencing it. They are peppered throughout the notes I wrote and, sometimes, themselves prompted me to write a note. I hope that after you finish each chapter you look again at its quotation and reflect on how it might connect to your own journey.

Annie "*understood the importance of preparation and information. Even things, especially things, we didn't really want to know.*"

A Better Man
Louise Penny

Introduction

I remember the call as if I made it yesterday. It was Thanksgiving weekend 2013, and while my partner of almost 25 years was at church I called my sister, Kris, to share devastating news. My voice cracking, I told her the diagnosis from ME's recent neuropsychological tests: Mild Cognitive Impairment (MCI). I explained that most people with MCI eventually develop Alzheimer's. At some point, I tearfully said that I already had concluded ME was not up to Christmas in Scotland, a family celebration in the works for more than a year. When Kris asked how I was doing, I said simply, "I want to run away."

It was the answer I gave frequently over the coming weeks. But I did not run away. Ultimately I ran down, however, MCI morphing into the dementia that steadily encroached on our lives. I did not realize it at the time, but as I stumbled into caregiving I was losing myself. My focus at first was on ensuring that ME got medical attention. I understood that the trajectory of her disease moved in only one direction and had its own timeline. For our immediate future, I anticipated a new normal; retirement would not be as carefree as we hoped. But we could continue to live our lives and enjoy ourselves. Until we couldn't.

Whatever I envisioned in late 2013, I know without a doubt that it did not include writing a book exploring the "gifts" my partner's dementia has given me. Being a caregiver is never easy, but the toll dementia exacts is most intense. I would come to learn that caregivers of people with dementia are seven times more likely than other caregivers to experience daily physical, emotional and mental exhaustion from caregiving. How then, you wonder, could anyone expect to find anything positive in the experience? How could any good emerge as a loved one disappears? I am telling my story to demonstrate possibility. I am telling my story — a story of love, discovery, grief, acceptance, hope and resilience — to show a path toward accepting that dementia need not claim two victims. I am telling my story because I have learned that living my best life does not mean I have abandoned my partner.

My story needs to be read as just that: mine. It is not a prescription for happiness or a guidebook or a caregiving manual. It is one caregiver's reflections, and she hopes you are inspired to make time for your own reflections. Perhaps in my story you will find reassurance and solace.

I have been told that the equanimity I have achieved is rare. That also motivated me to share my journey. Although there is a plethora of information for caregivers, I believe that the more individual stories are shared, the richer and more nuanced our understanding of caregiving becomes. The earlier one realizes there is no one "right" way to walk the path of caregiving, the easier life can be.

I made my share of mistakes as a caregiver, and I do not shy away from sharing them. I hope my hard-earned perspective offers a different way of framing the caregiving experience. If my story helps you know that you are not alone, relieves an anxiety, provides a chuckle, offers a glimmer of hope for a brighter tomorrow, I will have succeeded. And ME's dementia will have been the source of yet another gift.

"The one thing I know for certain . . . is that one word doesn't begin to sum [up a life]. . . . [T]he story of a life is nothing compared to a life."

Nuala O'Faolain
The Story of Chicago May

CHAPTER 1

Our "Befores"

In my dedication in the academic book we co-authored, I wrote that ME "daily renews my faith in goodness and constantly dazzles me with her brilliance." Of myself, I might write "kind and smart, but not in her league." Perhaps that is all the context you need to understand the devastation of her dementia, but I don't think those observations are enough to undergird the story of my journey. So indulge me while I tell you something about each of us and about us.

In every life, there is a variety of "before" and "after" defining moments. Before Diagnosis and After Diagnosis are at the heart of this story, but as I reviewed our histories I realized there have been many befores and afters. I also found numerous "shared" experiences that I had not previously connected.

ME is a child of WWII, born in May 1941. I am an early Baby Boomer, born in January 1949.

ME was raised Catholic; four uncles were priests. I was raised Lutheran;

a choir-director uncle was viewed by the congregation as a pillar of the church.

ME grew up in western Massachusetts, the second of four children and the only girl. I grew up in northeastern Wisconsin, the oldest of three.

ME was educated in Catholic schools. I attended public schools.

ME's father owned a small variety store with a soda fountain; her mother was a college graduate. My father was a bookkeeper; my mother had some "nurse's training" but left school after eloping.

ME grew up amid tragedy, and the death of her older brother from polio in 1953 was her first — and arguably most significant — Before/After. I have generally felt as if I lived a charmed life, but I had my own significant Before/After when I was molested by a high school teacher.

ME was salutatorian of her high school class, graduated from the same small Catholic women's college as her mother, taught second grade for a year, entered a convent, left before final vows, earned master's and Ph.D. degrees in sociology, joined the faculty of the University of Rhode Island in 1973, and retired from there in 2003.

I was a speaker at both my eighth-grade and high school graduations, graduated with honors in journalism from a state college in Wisconsin, and immediately escaped to the Pacific Northwest to earn a master's degree (in nine months, because that is all I could afford). I worked as a reporter at a small daily newspaper in central Wisconsin, then as an editor at a somewhat larger daily in northern Illinois before joining the faculty of the School of Journalism at the University of Missouri. I was 25. My academic career path was unusual: three years at Missouri, three years at my undergraduate alma mater, four years back at Missouri (where I was just the ninth woman to earn a Ph.D. in journalism and where I earned tenure), five years at the University of Hartford (hired without tenure, I declined to pursue it when the time came), and finally retiring in 2012 after 23 years at the University of Rhode Island (with a detour to a deanship at a small Massachusetts college for a year).

ME was a caregiver most of her life. Watching over her younger brothers as her parents coped with the death of their son. Minding her mother after the sudden death of her father in 1968. Choosing URI to remain geographically close to her mother, and assuming care for her mother as she descended into dementia. Nursing me through a severe case of Lyme disease and later a breast-cancer scare. Overseeing the care of a faculty colleague with ALS until his death. Befriending countless students, colleagues and friends in difficult times big and small.

I was painfully uncomfortable with the idea of caregiving. Family members often joked that I wanted to be a doctor, but didn't like sick people, so I earned the title with my doctorate degree. Decades later, at an introductory meeting with a home-care agency director, I began by declaring, "Caregiving is not in my wheelhouse!"

ME came to feminism at URI; she was the only woman in her 18-member department when she arrived. Years later, she was quoted in a newspaper story saying that was one of the factors that led to her "gradual awakening" to the problems women faced. That story called her the prime mover and researcher behind a class-action suit alleging the university discriminated against women in hiring, promotion, tenure and salary. It took ten years, but the suit was successful. ME also was a founding mother of the Women's Studies program at URI, eventually directing it for 15 years.

I did not know it at the time, but my feminism took seed when an uncle asked my parents, "Why is Barbie wasting money going to college? She'll just get married." I never looked back after taking the first women's literature and black literature courses offered at my college. Opposition to the war in Vietnam cemented my political activism, which included anti-war marches and testifying at a congressional hearing. My commitment to feminist issues grew with my career. I vividly remember my MG breaking down on the way home from an ERA rally. I still bristle as I recall an editor telling me to not be so "strident" about sexism in the newsroom and the news. Eventually I designed and taught courses on women and media, researched images of women in the media, and advocated for women's studies on my campuses.

Women's Studies brought ME and me together in the summer of 1989, when I joined the URI faculty as chair of the Journalism Department. When interviewing for the job, I told the dean I would want to be involved in Women's Studies. That's how I came to find myself in ME's office on August 31. (I know that because I found it in her datebook — with my last name misspelled.) We chatted as new colleagues do, sharing bits of professional and personal information. I learned she had spent the spring semester on sabbatical in Ireland, doing research on women in the Republic and gathering information for a new course on women in Irish society. I don't recall what I told her about myself, but I know we agreed to have lunch in the future. It is safe to say that neither of us foresaw the future that developed. Quickly.

Life together was full. It was ordinary. It was extraordinary. We enjoyed professional success. We enjoyed our home, our neighbors, our gardens, our friends. There were Women's Studies potlucks and parties. Our Christmas trees and decorations brought great joy, and at least one laugh (I still believe we are probably the only people to have returned a cut tree; we tried three stands and could not make it fit!). We regularly vacationed on Cape Cod. A visit to Hilton Head for spring break in 1991 led to annual trips there; for the longest time I called it my favorite spot in the world. We discovered Tucson and Green Valley, Arizona, because of former colleagues of ME. Professional trips took us to places such as Washington, D.C., Ames, Iowa, and Albuquerque, N.M. The graduations of nieces and nephews found us in Annapolis, Durham, N.H., Syracuse, N.Y., Madison, Wis. and Bristol, R.I. A wedding in Colorado allowed me to show ME the Boulder area I knew from vacations and for us to explore Denver. Another wedding introduced us to Pittsburgh. We travelled to Alaska — twice. I shared "my" Sparhawk resort in Ogunquit, Maine, and ME shared "her" Berkshires in western Massachusetts. We enjoyed attending women's volleyball and basketball games at URI. We were lucky to attend several Women's Final Fours and see incredible teams, including UConn, the University of Tennessee, Notre Dame, Stanford and Baylor. We played golf, actually lugging clubs to Hilton Head, Prince Edward Island and Nova Scotia. We enjoyed movies, concerts, art museums, restaurants and more. We devoured books.

ME was a homebody, but my restlessness won out more often than not. ME was uncomfortable with "aloneness" while I have an independent streak a mile wide. That proved both a help and hindrance to me as her mother's dementia progressed and her care more and more consumed ME.

I never said it — communication not being my strong suit — but always felt that her priorities were mother, work, us. I, on the other hand, was an "absent" daughter. I had lived at a distance since graduating from college, so emotional distance was easier. My father had a debilitating stroke in 1987, and for the most part the support I provided my mother and him over the 15 years she cared for him was financial. My priorities were work, us, family.

ME's mother died in 2001, and ME retired two years later, having given herself time to figure out that it was not just caring for her mother that had exhausted her, but also her job. A couple years later, she was once more a caregiver, coordinating help for our friend with ALS. She did so the only way she knew — all in. I found myself again feeling that someone else came before me (we could not even get away for a weekend without her getting a phone call that required her immediate attention). But whatever lessons I had learned about communication in therapy were forgotten; I said nothing.

We moved forward, even if on autopilot. I continued to work, invigorated by new responsibilities as the NCAA Faculty Athletics Representative for URI. I got to travel, especially after I was appointed to national committees. I enjoyed the work and — yes — the time alone. I don't remember much about what ME did, beyond the occasional lunch with former colleagues, lots of reading and household tasks. During school breaks and in the summers, we traveled, spent time with family and friends. One year morphed into the next. I envied ME's retirement; I was ready to do "what I want when I want."

When our financial advisor showed me I could retire and be unlikely to run out of money even if I lived to be 99, I danced around the house singing "Yippee." Not long after, I submitted the paperwork to call it quits in July 2012. Not for the first time did the disparity in our ages surface. (It always brought me up short to remember that when she graduated from college in 1963, I was graduating from eighth grade.) I had for a number of years confided to friends that I wanted to retire while ME was still "young enough" for us "to play." It turned out I was almost too late

*"We each write the story of our lives
one choice at a time."*

CHAPTER 2

The Crash

Early January 2012 found us in Fort Myers Beach, Florida, celebrating my sister's retirement. We three enjoyed a condo directly on the beach and beautiful weather that allowed for plenty of touristy activities. I remember (as does Kris) how upset ME was that the safety chain on the door was broken. She was so anxious about it that we humored her by propping a chair under the doorknob at night. At the time, I recall, I was aggravated by that anxiety but took it in stride.

On February 28, I turned in my retirement paperwork. Thus, our March trip to Green Valley, Arizona, was my last Spring Break getaway. We again enjoyed a comfy condo, gorgeous weather and our favorite Arizona activities, which included time with ME's former colleague Peg. ME, never a comfortable flier, was a bit clingy on the long trip west, but I had not thought a lot about it. I did think a bit more about a telephone conversation between her and Peg to arrange an outing after Peg immediately called me to make certain ME had gotten the details correct.

Early June brought ME's 50th college reunion, which she had been anticipating for some time (its magnet remains on our fridge). She had arranged to drive the 70 miles to Worcester, Massachusetts, then travel to Chicopee with her longtime friend, Joan. I remember ME being reservedly excited to connect with classmates and teachers, but more than a little apprehensive about driving to Worcester (a trip I daresay she had made at least a hundred times). I remember writing out the directions for her as a backup.

My retirement became official on June 30. To revisit the months immediately after that, I had to search my photos, calendars and notes. Without them, I remember only cleaning out my office — tossing files and outdated textbooks — and packing files and memorabilia; arranging to move my antique roll-top desk home; and an NCAA meeting in Indianapolis. I could not quite let go of my Athletics involvement, but an attempt to negotiate a part-time appointment fell through. Otherwise, I was happy to leave the grind that academia had become.

Turns out it was the summer of our first trip to Tanglewood (for "Prairie Home Companion") after years of saying, "We need to do that." It was the summer ME's beloved uncle Bill died; luckily we had gone to Atlantic City in time for her to visit him. It was the summer my nephew Bill received his master's degree from The Fletcher School at nearby Tufts University, with family stories all involving the July heat and humidity and our house's lack of air conditioning. It seems to have been the summer that our friend Sandra and I began meeting for our "techie coffees" (that eventually morphed into perhaps my most important lifeline). And it was the summer we last visited ME's 90-something second cousin in Plattsburgh, New York. As always, we found her "sharp as a tack" and marveled at that.

The only retirement "plan" I had made was to be out of Rhode Island on September 5, when classes would begin at the University. My idea had been to find an inviting destination within driving distance that neither ME nor I had visited. That had proved difficult, given ME's Massachusetts roots and our penchant for New England travel. Eventually I settled on Cooperstown, New York, for the National Baseball Hall of Fame and other attractions. (ME had been, but decades earlier.) Again I found her "clingy," always close at hand on our visit to the Fenimore Museum of Art and as we ambled about the grounds of the Farmer's Museum, and anxious as we drove unknown country roads. But again I thought little of it; perhaps I had become accustomed to those behaviors.

One year after that celebratory trip, our world turned upside down. Or was it inside out? Only in retrospect have I realized that some of the uneasiness I felt the previous year and periodically in 2013 probably was ME's disease taking root. I know I mentioned to Sandra that I had noticed "cognitive issues," that I found myself more and more saying, "I need a noun" (always eliciting a chuckle from ME). I remember ME returning home from a doctor's appointment and proclaiming out of the blue, "[He] says I don't have Alzheimer's." I just cannot pin down the exact "whens." Has there ever been a caregiver who has looked back and honestly could say, "I never saw it coming"?

"The crash" was sudden. Frightening. Discombobulating. Those were my immediate feelings. I don't know how ME experienced it, because we never discussed it rationally. It was Friday night, October 11. We were at the Hilton Garden Inn in Fredericksburg, Virginia, on our way home after two weeks in Hilton Head. Often, this stop would have meant dinner with friends from Arlington, but because it was a weeknight we were on our own. We had a quiet meal in the hotel. I remember ME having a difficult time deciding what to order, but that was not an unfamiliar situation. (A perfectionist, even what seemed to me a simple decision, like choosing a lemon at the market, could take her minutes.) I was exhausted from having driven every mile that day. I suspect we turned off the TV early because we would try to hit the road by 7:30 a.m. Sometime after midnight, ME bolted up in her bed, woke me, and in a panic said, "We have to get home!" In a grumpy fog, I responded: "It's the middle of the night. Go back to sleep. We'll be home tomorrow." She insisted that we had to leave immediately, so I opened the drapes, showed her it was dark and told her we would leave "when it is light."

What was happening? I didn't know, but I am not at my best when rudely awakened. After I managed to get ME settled, I fell back into a restless sleep. We did leave at first light. I was uneasy at the wheel, but there was no mention of the night before. After a couple hours, when we made our usual stop at a Maryland rest area for a bathroom and breakfast, ME seemed a bit disoriented. That disorientation only worsened as the day progressed. She was certain I was driving the wrong direction. She was uncharacteristically agitated in the car. By the time we reached home in the late afternoon, she was totally confused about her surroundings. I was confused by her behaviors.

Crash.

On Sunday and again on Monday, ME remained disconnected from reality — my description. I called her doctor for an appointment. By this time, I had conjured a brain tumor or something else physical. I think we saw the doctor on Tuesday. ME went into the exam room alone, but the doctor soon fetched me. I explained what had been happening. She ordered bloodwork ("They will want to see that first"), to be followed by an MRI. Lastly, if necessary, would be a neurologist and testing, and she provided referrals. I tried to be reassuring to ME, who typically jumped from A to Z, i.e. to the worst-case scenario. "One step at a time," I counseled. "As the doctor said, it could be something as 'simple' as a vitamin deficiency of some sort." I was not yet considering dementia, by the way.

The tests progressed. Bloodwork was normal (a disappointment, because that seemed the least-threatening outcome). The first MRI did not seem to show any mass or blockages, but a second, with contrast, was ordered. Nothing substantially out of the ordinary. On to neurological testing, after a wait for insurance-company approval. We answered a lot of questions, then I left ME for the in-depth testing and evaluation. The paperwork stated it could take several hours; the doctor suggested it would be an hour. He was right. On our drive home, ME described some of the things she was asked to do. It all was, she declared, "stupid" and "a waste of time."

The results were available a week later. I picked up the report the day before Thanksgiving and suggested we wait to read it until after the holiday. (I never revealed that I had read it in my car outside the doctor's office. The findings left me numb.) When I finally gave ME the report, she read the first paragraph and threw the document on the floor. She never asked to see it again. We never discussed it. When the doctor gave it to me, he had said, "This gives you time to plan."

How do you plan when neither of you seems able to talk about "it"?

"Four statements that lead to wisdom: I was wrong. I'm sorry. I don't know. I need help."

Referenced frequently by the lead character
in Louise Penny's *Armand Gamache* mystery novels

CHAPTER 3

Year One AD

The days AD — After Diagnosis — were a blur. They remain so. If we had talked about what was happening, perhaps that would not be true. But that is my reality. I do remember taking charge — that is how I am, being most comfortable when I can *do* something. I now recognize that I took over too much too soon, denying ME the opportunity to do while she still was able.

I tackled the paperwork required of the travel insurance we had purchased for our Scotland trip (eventually fully reimbursed; ME was happy about that). I called my brother to bring him up to speed; in a subsequent email I wrote, "I remain sad beyond words at this turn of events." I asked my sister to tell my three nephews what was happening; I knew I was not up to talking with them without breaking down. Break down I did when I got this email from Bill, the one living in Scotland: "I struggled all morning trying to figure out what to write to you and I haven't really come up with anything. Of course we will miss your company here but, first and foremost, our thoughts are with you both and the health of your partner especially. I am incredibly saddened by this news. We want you to know that you both are loved deeply by our family and our thoughts are with you." Our families' support AD has been unconditional. They have been there with us and for us. They have been my sounding boards. They have supported every difficult decision I have had to make.

I also talked with a couple of my dearest friends. That was done with Saturday afternoon or Sunday morning phone calls while ME was at church. I don't remember thinking twice about sharing information she was unwilling to share. I needed to talk, to vent. I became adept at subterfuge. I was not proud of that, but in a way I already had begun taking care of myself.

ME's brother Mike and sister-in-law Caryl had urged me to go to Scotland and enjoy my family. That did not feel right, so I chose to not go. Nonetheless, I was hurt and resentful at the lost opportunity. I kept that to myself. We spent Christmas in Connecticut with ME's extended family, and aside from my hovering and whispered conversations about ME's health, the day was as chaotic and fun as ever. Coffee and conversation the next morning were just as loving. We also spent Christmas "in Scotland," my sister holding our photos front and center for the family's "ugly sweater" portrait, castle visits and more. Happily, we were able to Skype on Christmas morning, and I held it together until just before I hit the "end" key (sobbing publicly is not something I do).

With ME's consent, I made a mid-January 2014 appointment with a neurologist. He patiently explained memory changes. ME said she didn't believe any such things were happening, but she listened. He gently described how they would like to monitor her. She said OK. He told us about a medication that might slow the progression of changes. She said OK. Thankfully she liked him; even better, she really liked CR, the

Registered Nurse Practitioner with whom she (we) would meet regularly. I do remember that at that first meeting, in a baseline screening test, ME was asked to spell WORLD backward, and she rattled off the correct answer even as I was struggling to do so in my head. I was impressed. I was hopeful. CR's advice before we left: "Go about your days."

We tried to do that, even as we continued to avoid talking about the MCI diagnosis. ME masked her condition, though as it turned out not as well as she seemed to think. Kris came from Wisconsin for my 65th birthday, and she ensured it was celebratory (my choice of movie — "August Osage County" — notwithstanding). It was clear that things were unsettled, but we three behaved as if it were just another visit. A lot of the time, life did seem rather normal.

One day, for example, ME and I had lunch at a favorite restaurant, then went to Walmart for a cast iron Dutch oven before taking the "scenic route" home, with stops at Narragansett Beach and Point Judith. Another day her Massachusetts brother and his wife visited. With the traumatic Hilton Head trip too fresh, in my note of thanks I wrote that "I was especially glad to not attempt that much car time for her."

We made plans to attend a concert with friends and I began work on two editing projects and some research for a friend. I also cleared lots of snow. As I used the snowblower, I sometimes would see ME watching from the den or asking from the front door what she might do to help. I always said "nothing." Snow removal, ironically, provided me some "alone time."

Similarly, I found time for myself in the kitchen and began baking up a storm: scones, cookies, cupcakes, weekly bread. ME loved sweet treats, so I justified my baking as something I could do for her, not as a caregiver but as her partner, her helpmate. That was an important distinction to me. The only help I allowed her, when she asked, was the cleanup — and sometimes not even that.

Periods of "minor" confusion were becoming commonplace. ME took a phone call from our friend Sandra one afternoon as I was making dinner. In a subsequent email, I told Sandra that ME had been "really unclear on what you said." When Sandra apologized, I clarified that she had not made things confusing, but rather "the message was lost in translation." What surprised me when I found that email, however, was reading that I already was having qualms about leaving ME at home alone. "While I am eager to see [the film] 'Nebraska,' ME has not reacted positively to its previews. And although she told me I should go with you, I am not comfortable leaving her on her own."

Yet a week later, her cousin Jane talked with ME and reported that it had been a "good" conversation. I told Jane that made me "glad," but added: "It is difficult, because she describes her issue as not being able to remember names. Doesn't really seem to recognize the cognitive difficulties. Or other behavior changes."

Jane was in regular touch with ME; emails confirm that I often followed up to fill in the blanks. That's how I know she started Aricept in mid-January, tolerated the non-therapeutic dose, and was bumped up to 10 mg in mid-February. It's how I know that development had me feeling hopeful.

Like Jane, a few friends checked in with me regularly; a common question was what was I doing to get support for myself. "I got a sense that you're too isolated," wrote one after we had talked. I told her I had been given recommendations for support groups, "But I don't do groups. Though I may be forced to rethink that position." I never did.

By that time I also was exchanging emails with my Uncle Delbert, whose wife suffered from Alzheimer's and after some years at home was living in a nursing home. Here was someone, I quickly learned, who knew what I was dealing with. He had wisdom, which he shared willingly. I was, in retrospect, more honest with him than perhaps anyone else.

Less than three months AD, I told him: "I think I am still in the anger phase, though it is more and more sinking in that the memory stuff and cognitive stuff and behavior changes are her brain malfunctioning. Still, I hope the medication might relieve some of the anxiety etc. Ordinarily we would be looking forward to ten days or so in Green Valley, Arizona, in mid-March. But traveling right now is out of the question; so much confusion after the drive back from Hilton Head, and I just do not want to put her through that or have to deal with it again. We also are not making [our usual] Hilton Head reservation, though if it looks do-able, we will hope the house there is available and fly down."

Finally, I wrote: "As I told a good friend in a long conversation last weekend, I never ever wanted children because, I think, I recognized that I am not a caretaker and I don't want to be responsible for anyone else but me. Well, this must be some cosmic joke, a year into retirement, to find myself in this situation."

As promised, Delbert shared descriptions of his early experiences with my aunt. After reading the first installment, I dashed off a quick message of thanks and added, "It hits so close to home that at the moment I cannot respond. . . ."

I also was able to have brutally honest conversations with my oldest friend, Luise, an ordained minister with a background in counseling. In early March 2014 she wrote me a long email with a sample "first conversation between you and ME." She laid out these goals: "Start talking. Support ME. Open the door to conversation; it never again can be closed. Let ME know that you are in this situation with her. (Future conversations may say otherwise, but for a first conversation ME need not hold the burden that she is alone.)"

Luise prefaced the proposed conversation this way: "You and ME are suffering. You both are living in worries about the far future when the present and the near future is yet to be either fully understood by each of you individually or as a couple. Breathe for a while. Both of you are suffering and not talking . . . making everything more difficult. You have the courage to deal with the whole picture, one day at a time."

The next day she offered more advice: on the value of finding a group for ME and the importance of me sharing my observations with her doctor. Finally, she emphasized: "It's important that any conversations at this time focus on ME and not on you. YOUR TIME IS COMING. THERE IS NO NEED FOR YOU TO LIVE YOUR LIFE TRAPPED. THAT WOULD NOT BE GOOD FOR EITHER OF YOU."

How do I describe the paralysis I felt when contemplating following through with such conversations? Even today I do not understand my visceral fear of confronting the reality that ME did not want to confront. Perhaps as long as we did not talk, I would not run away from us. I also see now that in our silences, each of us was lonely in our own ways. ME went regularly to the market and the pharmacy; the clerks, she told me, were her "friends." I retreated into household chores and gardening.

Although ME a few times remarked to me, "when I am better," she did not talk about her health with others. That something was amiss was apparent, however. In canceling an outing, I noted that "ME is dealing with some health issues (not life-threatening, but certainly life-changing)" — wording I used from that point forward. When a longtime colleague and friend of ME's asked another friend about her, and that friend alerted me, I suggested she call ME. "I am more comfortable letting ME speak for herself," I said.

And so we went about our lives. Outings with Sandra and Roberta, visits with Mike and Caryl, a memorial service for a colleague's mother, our first bat mitzvah, lunches out, etc. We enjoyed Easter with the family in Connecticut, attended a performance of "The Book of Mormon," went to Ogunquit, Maine, for our annual spring visit. But we attended only two women's basketball games (we were season ticket holders) because ME no longer could follow the game. And by May she no longer could manage email, so I regularly checked it for her. Of that trip to Maine, I told Sandra: "It went well. We were able to walk, shop and eat. Hung out in the evenings. ME didn't seem to have other than the usual confusion." I also mentioned that we were driving to Pittsfield with the cemetery flower boxes. "She says she is up to making the trip up and back in the day. We shall see."

I harbored hope we might return to Hilton Head when I updated "our" house's owner about ME's health. "Ya'll seem like family and I loved having you visit our home," she replied in late March. In June she wrote: "I am in HH sitting in Sun Room and I just thought of you and ME. Hope all is going well for both of you. Still hoping you will get to take your annual trip to HH which would mean ME's health is good!!! Doesn't seem right when I look at latter summer months and you are not on the calendar. Keep in mind if your situation changes I will certainly make room for you."

The situation changed, if imperceptibly, as 2014 moved along. In May, Luise, the friend who had written me so wisely about communication, came to Rhode Island for a week so we could work on her book (which I was editing). Prior to the visit, she asked about spending time alone with ME. "I think ME would enjoy a walk," I answered. "But please know that she does not know how much I have told you. I leave it up to her about self-disclosing, except for a couple of my close friends and family, to whom I can vent." Despite Luise's own health issues, we persevered in our work. ME and I also were able to show her a bit of the state, feed her seafood and share laughs. She and ME had private conversations, and their shared spirituality buoyed ME. Photos taken at the bus depot before Luise headed to Logan Airport show us all smiling broadly.

Yes, life had changed, but we adjusted and carried on — without really talking with each other about those changes. For me, that meant keeping some things "secret" as long as possible. For example, I "conspired" with Kris to get an appointment with a tattoo artist for when ME and I would be in Wisconsin in July. I had gotten a temporary tattoo at the bat mitzvah, liked seeing it on my forearm, and decided to get a real one. I knew I wanted a sunburst, and after some searching decided on the sun/moon design on a pin ME had given me. I thought to myself that it meant ME would always be with me. But I knew she would oppose the tattoo so, as I wrote Kris, I decided to tell her "as we walk out the door. Otherwise, she will likely fixate on it." And by "we," I meant Kris and I; no way would I bring ME.

Travel with ME always had made me a tad apprehensive, her trepidation and anxiety spilling over. Now I was anxious on my own, worried about how she would react in the car or, getting ready for Wisconsin, on a plane. I described the trip to my uncle as "an experiment to see how ME does with flying and being away [for a week]. I know long driving trips are in the past, but am hopeful this goes OK. Because I sure want to go to Hilton Head."

The trip proved to be more of a test than an experiment. Our 5 p.m. flight out of Providence ended up being cancelled — long after friends had dropped us at the airport and we were settled at the gate — because of storms to the west. We had no choice but to rebook for early the next morning; we were lucky that our friends were able to return to the airport to fetch us. Luckier still, Sandra agreed to take us to the airport at 4 the next morning. That flight to Chicago actually landed 20 minutes early, but it was downhill from there and we arrived in Oshkosh three hours late. Not for the first time — or the last — my efforts to reduce stress points for ME had been in vain.

Responding to this story, my friend Sue, whose book I had finished editing earlier in the year, advised me to find a support group. "While our experience is NOT the same, bearing witness to C's Mom's decline was tough. My recommendation to you is to find a support group, if you haven't already. I think that context would have helped us a lot. I know it would have helped C's sister, who was in the trenches . . . . Alas, hindsight is 20/20. Getting outside support with care and meals is smart, too. There is your wear and tear and stress levels to remember in all of this."

I passed on that wise advice. I passed on my annual Sisters' Week trip to Wisconsin for a Packers game, too. But I took a gamble and decided not to pass on a trip to Peru in January 2015. As my sister put it, this was to be our delayed "trip out of your comfort zone."

I had survived being out of another kind of comfort zone when ME had cataract surgeries in September and October. I learned the value of a medical Power of Attorney. I also became an expert at administering eye drops, the schedule and task too much for ME. That caregiving felt temporary, however, and I did not identify myself as a caregiver. If I was lurking at the edges of web sites about dementia and Alzheimer's, I jumped off them quickly. We weren't talking about that and I wasn't ready to really confront reality.

In between surgeries, ME's visit with the neurologist had been "positive," so that is when I broke the news about Peru. ME's response was subdued. I emailed Kris that the trip was "a go." A subsequent email recounts what came next: "At least it was calm for a while. But after I had fallen asleep that night she woke me to say it just had dawned on her what it meant that I had told her in the afternoon. She was upset that I had not talked with her first, just told her, and didn't even ask if she wanted to go. I rolled over and faked sleep, figuring I would let her sleep on it. Still pissed in a.m. I tried to explain why I had done it that way, knowing as soon as I said anything it would cause anxiety. Oh well. No fireworks since. . . . Caryl has said they will do whatever, so probably will try to arrange so ME mostly stays at home. Glad there are many weeks before we go."

Later that October, one of ME's nieces in Massachusetts was getting married. I feared the three-hour drive to ME's hometown, which she had made hundreds of times, could be trouble. Ditto a night in a motel. But the trip went about as well as could be expected, with me hyper-vigilant and sensitive to how much activity ME was comfortable with. When the music got loud and the dancing began, we said our goodbyes. I could tell that people understood; I don't think ME was aware that they were aware of her situation.

We were up early the next morning, went out for a quick breakfast and headed home after a stop at the cemetery. I described the trip this way to Jane: "We had a generally pleasant ride across Massachusetts on Route 9 hoping to see some color. ME did pretty well, though some confusion at times over geography."

Jane replied:

> It was good seeing you. You both looked great. . . . I am hoping we can get together for a day or two. After seeing ME, I am worried about her. I knew things were not going well but I definitely got a clearer picture at the wedding. . . . Just so you know, Michael told me that ME would be staying with him while you are [in Peru]. (By the way, he called you a saint!) I know any changes for ME will be difficult but you need to get a break and have some fun!!!! Relaxation, you know, is very important, especially to a caregiver. . . . I am sure she would prefer you to be with her but [the family] will make her comfortable and feel at home.

A few weeks later, ME and I made our annual fall visit to Ogunquit, which also went "pretty well," even with a couple days of rain, I told Jane. It had been "just good to get away. We have a routine of places we go and things we do, and I think that helps. Though increasingly ME responds to things as if it is the first time." Those emails were among the first of dozens Jane and I exchanged over the years, a treasure-trove of good advice for me and love for ME.

Suddenly Thanksgiving approached and we had survived the first year AD. Much about our lives was unchanged: ME was still driving, albeit only around town. We ate out. We went to movies. We enjoyed Sunday drives and Dairy Queen stops. We took walks, together or with our closest friends. We watched TV. We kept up with the news (I learned from Jane that at the wedding, ME had asked another cousin, who worked for an airline, about how it was dealing with the Ebola crisis.) We celebrated family birthdays and holidays. Despite the confusion I often saw, ME was generally self-sufficient. And I remained stubbornly independent.

At the same time, some things had changed. ME was more tentative. Decisions were even more difficult for her and she deferred to me more often. At restaurants, for example, I took to telling the server her order, careful to always say "ME will have. . . ." Increasingly she struggled with her checkbook, until she finally agreed to allow me to balance it for her. She seldom read, and even when she appeared to be engrossed in a book or the newspaper, she was just staring at a page. Sometimes she was a beat or two behind during conversations, making her point after the topic had changed. In my Thanksgiving email to Jane, I wrote: "Yes, it is difficult watching the decline. The memory loss is one thing, but it is the loss of cognitive stuff that is hardest to deal with. Some days are better than others — for both of us."

Just before Christmas I amplified those thoughts in an email to my uncle:

We saw the [neurological nurse practitioner] in November, and she documented some change. When she did the 20-question "test," ME missed four more than she had six months earlier. The one that jumped out at me was when they asked her to spell WORLD backwards. At the first appointment, I almost fell out of my chair when she cranked it out effortlessly. This time she never could do it. They want to add a medication they say is supposed to bolster the Aricept. But it is not available right now. So she has an appointment for February and they expect to have it then.

What I notice are all the "little" changes in daily life, the things that are more difficult and/or impossible for her to do without my help. The occasional mood change or weirdness, too. With golf over for the year, I basically only get out of the house to shop or run an errand or now and then have coffee with a friend. Very hard for me, because I always have needed my space and my time.

Still, ME continued to be quite adept at "masking" her cognitive difficulties. And a year into the journey, I still was not identifying myself as a caregiver.

". . . Just because a subject is difficult to learn, it does not mean you are not good at it. You just have to grit your teeth and work harder to get good at it. Once you do, there's a strong chance you will enjoy it more than anything else."

Carolyn Turk
"My Turn" essay in *Newsweek*, April 5, 2004
Posted for years outside my office

CHAPTER 4

Turbulence

The holiday letter I sent in mid-December 2015 summed up our year thusly:

What a year, with weird weather at its start and finish. In January, I was able to get away to Peru for nine days, visiting my middle nephew and his wife, who teach at an international school in Lima. Along with my sister and two cousins, we went to Machu Picchu and Cusco, and I celebrated my birthday in the Sacred Valley. Alas, my plane was the last to land in Providence as New England's first blizzard kicked up. I spent too much of the next five weeks removing snow.

ME and I spent Easter week in Hilton Head, a spot that always renews me. Next up was gardening and golf, the latter keeping me smiling all the way through November. Alas, my schedule and the warm days of December have not matched up, though I still hope to fit in a round or two.

Time with family is always the best. July took us to Wisconsin, where I finally met my newest grandnephews, saw my sister and brother-in-law's 'up North' trailer, helped celebrate my oldest nephew's 40th birthday at an '80s-themed surprise party and my youngest nephew's 31st with a surprise dinner. Alas, my brother and 13-year-old niece could not get to Wisconsin until a couple weeks later.

Throughout the summer, ME and I used day-trips to explore Rhode Island parks, beaches and seafood restaurants. We enjoyed a day of racing at Saratoga, where the first horse I ever bet on WON. We also saw a lot of movies; remarkably, we agreed all of them were terrific. Alas, we qualify for the Wednesday senior citizen rate.

More family in October, after I made a late decision to return to Wisconsin to help my sister celebrate her 65th birthday. That we did with a fabulous meal at the historic Union Hotel in De Pere. Our Packers tix for the year went to middle nephew as his present for graduating from Top Gun school, so we were going to be the day's designated driver. Alas, at the last minute we scored tickets and enjoyed a win because of a heart-stopping defensive stand with the clock winding down.

And more family in November, when Kris and Fred drove out to share Thanksgiving. We had a grand old time eating lobster rolls (and more), visiting Plymouth (still amazed that we trace our roots to the Mayflower), seeing 'Spotlight' (makes me proud to be a journalist), shopping local and talking, talking, talking. Alas, they left us for a surprise visit to their grandchildren in Virginia. Go figure!

Finally, my Fitbit tells me almost every day that I have not walked enough, TripAdvisor tells me more than 51,000 people have read my reviews (probably more of an impact than any of my academic writing), and my Kindle attests to my binge-reading of J.A. Jance. Alas, I have enough unread books to get me through 2016 and then some. I trust that you, too, are well stocked — and stoked — for the new year.

Who reading that letter would ever have guessed the turbulence in our lives? That trip to Peru marked a significant turning point in my caregiver journey, but for the most part I kept that to myself. When I returned after 10 days away, it soon became clear to me that I indeed was a caregiver. Up to that point, my narrow definition required doing "personal care." I recognized that was my most significant fear, brought to the fore when I somewhere read, "Are you ready for fecal incontinence?" I knew personal care was in ME's future, but up until now I had seen myself as a "manager." I managed appointments and social engagements, offered assistance, provided guidance, assumed responsibility for most household tasks. Whenever family or friends remarked on my caregiving and patience, I dismissed that label.

As much as I felt my world altered AD, the Peru trip forced me to face the stark implications of ME's disease more directly. Throughout my life, I never felt adequate caring for anyone but myself (and I did not always do such a good job with that!). Being responsible for another person was a daunting task; there was a reason, after all, that I never wanted children.

I had not gone to Peru because Machu Picchu was on my "bucket list" (actually, I have no such list). I went because this was the trip "out of my comfort zone" I had promised to share with my sister. As a matter of fact, it was out of my comfort zone in the usual sense of the phrase and also because it meant leaving ME to stay with her brother and sister-in-law. Traveling without her was not an issue for me; I was unsure and nervous about how she and they would fare. But I was leaving it up to them to figure out, as I wrote in an email to her cousin Jane: "She won't be alone, but no doubt it will have its dicey moments." For me, the struggle was to not back out of what likely would be a once-in-a-lifetime adventure.

Planning the trip had not been easy. Initially, I kept its existence a secret. Once I told ME about the trip, I was both excited and apprehensive. I walked on eggshells, never knowing how she might react. "I hate that I cannot just take it all in stride," I told my sister. "Part of it is just me. Part of it is the situation with ME. At least she now brings up the trip, but [she has] so much confusion over when and for how long etc. I am trying to keep the details simple, but it does not matter. On top of everything, it is hard to find a few minutes of alone time. She has taken to a lot of hovering, reading over my shoulder, etc."

If I needed an affirmation of our new reality, it occurred on January 23, my birthday. We were in a colonial-era house in Cusco for three nights. We had spent the day sightseeing in the Sacred Valley and I had been treated to a birthday lunch at the Blue Llama, a quaint eatery in Pisac. Back at the house, I was able to FaceTime with Connecticut. ME was baffled by the entire experience of seeing me on the phone. We talked less than a minute. Afterward, in our room, my sister hugged me as through tears I lamented, "She didn't even know it was my birthday." In that moment I might as well have been an abandoned child, my feeling of loss was so great.

A few days later I headed back to Rhode Island, unsure of the reception that awaited me but sure of the gut-wrenching hurt that mixed with a deep love I had not felt much lately. I continued to travel outside my comfort zone, being on my own for the return trip. I also had to deal with a mighty blizzard bearing down on the Northeast. In order to avoid getting stuck in Rhode Island, Mike and Caryl had to leave ME home alone for what we thought would be a couple of hours. Our friends Sandra and Roberta would check on her and take her to get groceries. Tempering anxiety (that I would be stuck in an airport and ME would be alone at home) with my usual optimism, I bided my time at Reagan National, fueled by Starbucks. My flight from D.C. turned out to be the last to land before the Providence airport was closed. Sandra and Roberta were there to fetch me, with ME, and we made it home without incident and with much relief. I had left for the Lima airport about 10 the previous night, with temps in the high 70s; now it was about 7 p.m., with temps in the low 20s.

ME was quiet during the drive from the airport; I just held her hand. I most remember standing in the kitchen, hugging her as she sobbed, and realizing I could feel ribs and how surprised by that I was. Her crying also surprised me; amid the tears I sensed fear and confusion — and I felt helpless. I longed for a hot shower, which I followed with a slice of leftover pizza before we both crashed. I was asleep before 9. At some point I awoke briefly and turned off the TV. The wind was howling. We had kept the heat turned up overnight and in the morning kept our fingers crossed that we would not lose power. Welcome home, Barb.

When I was able to talk with Mike and Caryl, I learned just how confusing my time away had been for ME, who was convinced I had left her for good. I tried in those first days home to be reassuring, but I also confronted the growing realization that the equation of our partnership had altered permanently. The downward trajectory of her disease, which I had acknowledged from the beginning, indeed was progressing.

It turned out to be a winter from hell in more ways than that. "It seems like all I have done since my return is clear snow and ice and ferry ME to appointments. Or huddle under a warm quilt," I told a friend. Storms came in waves; our little snowblower got a workout. ME always volunteered to help by shoveling; I always encouraged her to stay inside and keep warm. As much as I hated the snow, dealing with it was an hour I had to myself. Besides, when she tried to help with anything, it doubled my work — and my aggravation!

I had hoped retirement would allow us to escape winter for longer than a week. Since that was not to be, Hilton Head in the spring would at least provide a short respite. Before I left for Peru, I had bravely confirmed a 10-day stay for early April, and even wrote our host, "ME says she is looking forward to Hilton Head, so that is a good thing." I also told her optimistically that I hoped we might be able to visit again in early October. Although I managed the details, I "allowed" ME to be part of the decision-making. The trip would be our longest time away in almost two years. We would fly to Hilton Head; no way did I want a repeat of October 2013.

In the meantime, I vowed to keep us busy. Being active allowed us to fall back into our habit of not talking about ME's health. That was our comfort zone. We met Mike and Caryl at the casino for lunch and penny slots. We enjoyed outings and meals with Sandra and Roberta. We went to a couple basketball games. I baked healthy bread, the scones ME loved for breakfast, cookies and brownies. I tried recipes from the Food Network shows we enjoyed watching. I also continued to resist her help with tasks like doing dishes or laundry or making the bed because it was easier to do them myself. I carved out moments for me by shutting her out. That was my "dirty little secret." My coping mechanism.

I had two other coping mechanisms. One was regular "conspiratorial coffee" with Sandra. I could vent — and vent some more. Sometimes she would vent. Almost always we bounced ideas off one another, she being perhaps the most creative person I know and me being an informed sounding board. My other coping mechanism was golf, especially the weekly drives to and from the course with Libby. She quickly transitioned from acquaintance to friend to confidante.

With Sandra, Libby and the other VIPs in my life, I shared my growing frustrations and anger, along with the mundane moments of life evolving ever faster. "I know it's the dementia," I would say, "but that doesn't make it any easier." I was careful to guard ME's privacy, but that wasn't always possible. Taking care of me sometimes required violating ME's boundaries.

At other times, taking care of me coincided with taking care of ME. A case in point was when she agreed to allow me to tackle "the landfill" that was her side of the bedroom. That was almost as out of character as allowing me the previous fall to clean out the garage and not objecting to anything I wanted to throw away. Including an old trunk that had sat unopened for at least twenty years. I should have realized then, but did not, that a change was under way in my partner the packrat.

The bedroom took me more than a week. I carried piles of papers, receipts, cards and the like down to the den and as we watched TV sorted them, mostly into recycle and shred piles. As I was sorting, ME kept saying that she did not know where "all that stuff" came from. When I said it was because she never threw anything away, she answered, "I didn't ask them to send it to me." Funny. And sad. Only after bare carpet surfaced could I dust and vacuum — not dust bunnies but dust rabbits, I joked. I also disposed of several boxes of books, some unread and never to be read. That made me sad. But it was rewarding to finish the work before we left for Hilton Head on April 5.

As with all our travels since October 2013, I managed all aspects of the trip. I got us packed, got the house buttoned up, kept a watchful eye on ME, ensured her needs were met and reassured her as necessary. If only I had been prescient a couple years earlier when, at Midway airport waiting for our flight to Providence, ME had me feeling as scared as I think I ever have been. We alternated going to the bathroom so the other of us could watch our bags at the gate. After a reasonable amount of time, ME did not return. I stood and looked around; no sign of her. The boarding lineup began. No ME. I couldn't leave our bags. I began to panic: Where the hell are you? No ME. I was frantic. Finally, seconds before we were to board, I spotted her, yelled to get her attention, then hurried us to our spot in line. She wondered why our gate had been changed (it had not). Clearly she had been wandering. She was not scared; she was angry at me for changing gates without her. Thankfully, our Hilton Head flights were uneventful.

Our ten-day stay was uneventful, too. And different. ME still enjoyed eating out at our favorite restaurants, doing a bit of shopping and walking the beach. But she did not join me at the pool; she locked herself in the house. I was able to play golf only because the course allowed her to ride in the cart with me. The day before we left, I wrote my uncle: "It has gone pretty well, but of course not necessarily as restful as I would like. Hard to see ME's confusions and unfamiliarity with places we have been for the last 25 years. But I am grateful to be here, to walk the beach, to sit on the deck or in the sunroom and read. I just have to hope this will not be our last visit."

Confusion. The old saw about distinguishing between not being able to find your car key and not knowing what the key is for sooner or later becomes startlingly real — for the person with dementia and those around her. We celebrated ME's birthday at home with Sandra and Roberta. I bravely tried two new recipes. We three had to repeatedly assure ME that yes, she really was 74, and yes, today really was her birthday.

We had gone to Ogunquit, which I first visited in 1971, shortly after our return from Hilton Head — problematic timing in an "ordinary" year. On the last of our three nights, I wrote to Delbert.

> I have been coming here regularly since about 1984, and for the last 25 years or so each spring and late October. Obviously, I love it — and Sparhawk, our lodging with a room fronting the ocean. Nice R&R, though so different an experience than just a few years ago. But ME is doing pretty well and we have managed to do the things we always have done. So I guess I need to be thankful for that and overlook all the things that make me crazy, at least some times. Patience is a virtue often in short supply.

As 2015 wore on, I was more and more conscious of ME's confusion. People would remark on my patience with her, and in public I really worked at preserving her dignity. In private, I often met her confusion with astonishment, silence or, worst of all, frustration and anger. That was particularly true when she managed her anxiety by staying close to me. For example, I wrote Luise that ". . . seldom do I get to open mail without ME hovering and questioning. Indeed, that is pretty much my life these days. And I resent the hell out of it more often than not." I did not, however, let my anger or her confusion dominate our lives. I made sure activity dominated. I have a photo book of the summer as proof, with its ironic cover lines:

> The sand may brush off
> The salt may wash away
> The tans may fade.
> But the memories will
> last forever.

I was learning to be satisfied with what we could have. We could "play" with friends, even though ME's engagement was unpredictable. We could eat out, even though ME might need help ordering and was unlikely to say much. We could go to movies, even though the days of spirited conversation were gone and ME was unlikely to offer much commentary afterward. We could enjoy walks and discover new spots, like Rocky Point, even though ME was likely to be a bit nervous. We could do family celebrations, even though ME probably would get antsy after a couple hours. "I try to stay positive about my life. Not always easy," I told Luise. It would be a long time before I identified this attitude as a gift, but it was.

Also a gift were the moments — captured in words or by a photo — when life seemed unburdened. I think here of a beautiful picture from our July trip to Wisconsin, of ME, my sister and my young grandnephew Connor. To look at a broadly beaming ME, one never would guess anything was wrong. When I stumbled on that photo doing research, it took my breath away. Such moments were rare, however. By late August I mentioned to Jane that ME "is not having a good day. Accused me of talking about her to everyone else." A few days later, we were waiting for ME's friend Joan to arrive for an overnight visit and birthday dinner. I explained to Jane that "ME seems very confused by it all. Not sure she fully grasps who Joan is. Asked me where she lives, if her parents are alive, and if we had ever been to her house. Scary. Seems to have been a major change over the last several days."

It was true that I talked about her situation, but only to a few people. If she were talking about it to anyone, I was not aware. And although I had grown used to dealing with her confusion, her questions about Joan threw me for a loop. An anecdote I recounted to Jane also was revealing. I emailed her while ME was at church, not wanting to fuel paranoia. We had met Mike and Caryl for lunch at the casino the day before.

> It was a nice little outing, despite a nasty crack or two about me by ME. But those things seem quickly forgotten or overlooked by her. I'm trying to learn just to ignore. You asked about changes, and that is one. Also seems to be more confusion/difficulty with ADLs [daily self-care activities]. And very little initiated conversation. She says basically nothing about her situation, though when I recently asked if she needed anything when I was out doing errands, she replied, "a new brain."

Jane's response offered me needed perspective:

> Paranoia is all part of the over-all problem. The reasoning skills are limited, so a sort of protective mode takes over. . . . This is new for ME but it isn't less frustrating. Were those nasty comments to get sympathy from M & C or just to 'punish you' for not jumping to her needs? or not being able to fix her? I know that she knows she is failing mentally and she can't control it. Does she ever refer to [her mother] and what she saw her going through or is that too touchy?

That may have been the first time I was aware that ME acknowledged her situation to someone else. I wrote back to Jane that I thought the nasty comments "were just lashing out at feeling picked on. Which of course was not the case." I added that she has not referred to her mother, "at least not her failing. Rather she will talk about her poetry or baking etc. I, on the other hand, make the comparison (in my head) all the time."

For some time, Jane had been urging me to get outside help, and offered good suggestions. I knew I was wearing down; indeed I was concerned that my upcoming wellness check would find issues with my blood pressure or cholesterol. And for several months my walking had been put on hold because of hip pain. But I also knew how badly ME wanted to remain at home (that was something made clear long before she became ill) and I was determined to honor that as long as possible. "I know we are moving toward [outside care]," I told Jane. "But ME has always been so private, and that is being magnified, that I have a hard time imagining her agreeing to it. So I put it off. I will plant the seed with Mike and Caryl," with whom she would stay during my five-day October trip to Wisconsin. "I know that when the time comes for personal care, I will have hit my limit. That is something I cannot do." Not for the first time did I make clear that my caregiving had limits.

As of yet, however, my commitment to keeping us active and involved seemed limitless. There was a three-day stretch where I had planned "adventures" for us each day. ME seemed to enjoy herself, perhaps because she had gotten ice cream each day. My cholesterol and blood pressure had been fine, so I felt emboldened to allow us to indulge. When heat and humidity were followed by gorgeous weather, I got us out of the house. We visited new spots around the state and others that we had not been to in years. "ME seems to enjoy that, though there is not much conversation," I wrote my uncle.

My quick trip to Wisconsin was to celebrate my sister's 65th birthday. The day before Mike and Caryl were to pick up ME and bring her to Connecticut, she was unusually anxious in the morning, but calmer when we headed out for a drive to see fall foliage and get lunch at an almost 100-year-old burger stand in Colchester, Connecticut. I travelled to Oshkosh with some anxiety of my own. I sensed it would be the last time I could ask Mike and Caryl to take ME. Although her stay went OK, it was in fact the last. I wondered how I would be able to travel.

Thanksgiving marked the end of Year Two AD. With winter approaching, I dreaded being more housebound, hoping the *Farmer's Almanac* prediction of severe cold and snow would be proven wrong.

". . . the dark fingers of dementia got her in their grip, and they pried loose random bits of her memory every day."

Susan Orlean
The Library Book

CHAPTER 5

Year Three AD

I know all too well that time — and trauma — can erase one's memory bank. I remember so little about my high school years that I rely on my sister for details. As for 2016, it proved to be the year on this journey that I remembered least. I didn't know that when, at the end of the year, I told friends Sandra and Roberta that "I would offer to bring something [for our holiday dinner], but I got nothing." Turned out I wasn't just talking about food. I was physically and mentally spent. I was a caregiver running on empty.

I can write about that year only because I discovered an active email life that recorded much of our day-to-day activities, dementia's downward spiral and my growing frustrations and uncharacteristic temper. I even unearthed the occasional reference to ME's reaction to her situation. Those were rare, however, because she continued to reference "when I get better" and we continued to *not* talk about IT.

This new year started with me optimistic about us traveling to Hilton Head in the spring, despite ME's continuing decline, which I mentioned to Luise early in January as we resumed work on her book. I always have described myself as a "born optimist," and somehow I did not totally lose that on this dementia journey. I knew from the beginning that the disease was in charge and had its own timetable. Nonetheless, I challenged it every day (subconsciously, for sure) by trying to keep us active and engaged. I worked hard at protecting ME and providing us "normalcy." I wanted ME to be out and about. I wanted her to experience life. I wanted to postpone the inevitable — as I expected it — as long as possible. Family and friends complimented me about this. As one who does not believe in regrets, I said time and again that "I don't want to leave anything on the table." Of course, in keeping ME busy I also could be out in the world. I was less lonely. I was intellectually challenged. I was entertained. I could even relax a bit.

At least at the beginning of the year, I remained comfortable leaving ME home alone for short periods of time. That meant I could do physical therapy (for a painful back/hip issue, which I think was at least in part a "resting place" for stress). It meant I could run errands when she did not want to come (or I preferred she not come). It meant I could run out to pick up a pizza. I also was able to drop her at church and enjoy 45 minutes to myself before picking her up. I did not realize what a gift that time was until long after I no longer had it.

I am amazed how many movies we saw that year. I wonder now how much ME got out of them. Did she understand "The Danish Girl," for example? We saw it with Sandra and Roberta, but as I recall we three dissected it at dinner afterward and ME was mostly silent. I certainly missed her commentary on movies — and the news, politics and so much more. My sadness for her as her intellectual capabilities deserted her was profound.

I counted on us getting out for the senior matinee on Wednesdays, especially when winter kept us cooped up. My emails often referenced weather (I think of my Dad and how most of my adult conversations with him started with the weather). I was happy to have our little electric snowblower, but I hated having to use it. And I desperately wished to live where I did not need a set of clothes used only for snow removal. "Arghhh. Hating winter," I wrote Luise in mid-January. A day later I shared a detailed report with Sandra, who was enjoying mid-60s in Florida and due home in a couple days. "The TV people are going wild," I told her. "Way too early to tell; system still off Pacific Northwest. What they are suggesting at the moment is that the storm center will be to the south of us and the Mid-Atlantic will bear the brunt. Timing sounds more Saturday, but again too early to tell. At least [one TV weatherman] said we will have real data in 24 hours and things then can start to shape up. What you gonna do?" I went on to tell her that the "wind has been howling for the past 24 hours." That did not stop me from taking us to Sam's Club to buy coffee before the store closed for good, and to hope we could see "Carol" the following day. We did, and I had one word for it: "Wow!"

Then we hunkered down for the storm. We skipped a luncheon and basketball game, to avoid being out at the blizzard's beginning. I assured Sandra that I had "a roast for the crockpot and the ingredients to make German Chocolate Cake bars. Also lots of movies on the DVR. And I am reading a good book." It was January 23, my 67th birthday. I know that only because in an email to Luise I mentioned the "blizzard raging outdoors," adding: "Birthday girl struggles with sadness over lack of birthday acknowledgement in the house. She will get over it."

I guess I did. Two days later I wrote my niece-in-law Shelly about our 12 inches of snow and drifts, being shoveled out by our lawn guy's daughters so I only did an hour of "touching up," and remarkably commented: "It is amazing to watch angry people in TV news stories, who cannot seem to comprehend the enormity of dealing with that amount of snow. I say go with the flow, so to speak, and enjoy the sparkling blue sky this morning (here, anyway)." ME's illness was proving to be a source of perspective for me. When you're dealing with dementia, nothing else quite measures up on the misery scale.

It didn't take much to draw out my optimism, either. A week later I updated Shelly. Our snow had more or less disappeared. When I went out for the newspapers, it felt — and looked — like spring. Just one small snow pile remained in the front yard. And it was raining. It felt raw, and I decided we would skip that night's women's basketball game. My, how things had changed for us. There was a time when nothing would keep me from a game, and ME gladly joined me. Now she no longer could follow the action and I embraced any little "inconvenience" in order to stay home — the easy way out.

So, I told Shelly, "lots of TV, because it occupies ME. She does not read much anymore, except for glancing at the paper. Sad. We did get out yesterday to meet a friend for lunch. It was so sunny, I suggested a bit of a drive, which was nice. She enjoys that. I am hopeful that when the weather gets nice, we might find a weekend to fly down [to Virginia] for a visit." Ah me, ever the optimist.

The day before Valentine's I awoke in a funk, explained only in part by having had to deal with yet another storm just a few days after rain had washed away the previous snow. By now I was spending time almost daily on Luise's manuscript. We Skyped frequently and emailed in between. Something she had written the night before cheered me, which I shared with her as I described my manic morning: "I did awake about 4, but managed to doze some until close to 6. Spent the morning in the kitchen: baked oatmeal, which will give me breakfasts for the week, and Red Velvet cupcakes. Frigid outside, so we stayed home and watched westerns on TV as I edited your manuscript. It's real!"

My sleeping habits had been unsettled almost since ME's diagnosis. A generally great sleeper for most of my life, I had turned into a restless sleeper and an early bird. I have tried to make peace with that more times than I can count, but I do not like it. I can explain it, though. The more ME's dementia progressed, the less alone/quiet time I had. She continued to sleep well, so by getting up at 5 or 6 (sometimes earlier), I almost always was guaranteed a couple hours to enjoy my coffee and read for pleasure. Mostly I devoured fiction, but I also was fond of the book-length journalism/nonfiction that I had taught in my "literature of journalism" course. My middle nephew, Nick, and I used the Voxer app to have long discussions about books and to make recommendations to one another — a two-person book club. I often saved his Voxes for the morning, so I could start my day hearing a friendly voice.

What I did not read were books (or magazine and newspaper articles) about caregiving, dementia or Alzheimer's. That may seem counterintuitive, given my preference for learning by reading. I don't think I was being arrogant; I think I was afraid of what I would learn. I wasn't ready for the information. So in my research for this book, I was astounded to discover that I had bought *Into the Storm: Journeys With Alzheimer's* just three months after ME's diagnosis. I recalled reading a review of it and ordering it for my Kindle, then leaving it there untouched. When did I finally read it? I don't know for sure, but it was not for a least a couple years AD.

The reading time I carved out for myself in the mornings helped me cope with the rest of the day. So did baking. I made my first pie — pumpkin — and it tasted pretty good. Yet the act of making it also was bittersweet, because ME had been the pie maker in our family. Trying new recipes was another coping mechanism. ME enjoyed the Food Network shows as much as I, perhaps remembering years (before us) when she had been part of a gourmet dining group. And the Y, which I had joined at the start of physical therapy in order to ride a recumbent bike for exercise, helped me cope when our walks were curtailed.

I elaborated on these when I caught up with ME's cousin Jane in late February, an email that was part news and part venting:

> You ask how it is going and my answer would be — one day at a time. There are lots of changes, but maybe only I notice. And of course it is not linear. But in general, there is little offered conversation. And little affect. For example, when I told her of my cousin's death, it was as if I told her it was snowing. She seemed to have little awareness about Xmas. And my birthday and Valentine's Day came and went without comment.

> So far, at least, I still can go out for a while without too much trouble. . . . But one morning I was gone a couple hours and when I came home she was convinced that the people on TV

were real and were in the house. Winter is more difficult, of course, because it often is harder to be out and about. But we try to go to a movie every week or so. ME seems to enjoy them, though I'm not sure how much she can follow the story. We went to a concert with friends and again, she seemed to enjoy it. I hope to take us to Hamden next week to see an exhibit at the Irish Famine Museum and have lunch with Caryl and Mike.

I could be happy when I could make ME happy. So it was on the last day of February, one of the warmest Februaries on record, when we went for a drive and discovered that "our" Dairy Queen had reopened. We enjoyed our first Blizzards of the season, with a photo to mark the occasion. But I needed more emotional rewards than that.

I always left the Y telling myself "Good girl" because I knew I had done something important for me. After completing a particularly challenging task with Luise's manuscript, her comments reminded me that I was more than a caregiver: "Well, I don't believe in perfection. Your blending of these stories brings the word 'awe' to my mind and heart. How do you blend two stories without one ragged phrase or sentence? This piece feels so right and accurate. 'Hit the ball right on the head' or some such saying, says it all. You are remarkable."

Kitchen successes were equally important for my ego. For example, for Easter with Mike and Caryl and extended family, I decided to make Red Velvet cupcakes with frosting that looked like grass, because I had decided it was time to learn how to use a piping bag. Ha! My big mistake at JOANN's was not asking for help, so I did not have a coupler (although I did buy coupler rings!) and the 10-inch bag was probably not the best choice. My mistake at home was frosting that probably should have been a tad thicker. "Despite all that," I wrote a friend, "I am proud that this old dog still can learn a trick or two."

Most affirming of all, however, were the regular coffee/conversation hours I spent with Sandra and the regular outings and meals we shared with her and Roberta. The coffees allowed me space to vent and lament, and helped me maintain my emotional equilibrium. Couples time was what we had been sharing since 1990, albeit evolving with ME's status. What a gift to have friends who, as I tried to do, accepted what was without expectation. What a gift it was that we continued to be included.

S: "We just bought tickets for Cheryl Wheeler at the Courthouse Center for the Arts. Are you interested?" I asked ME, she said yes, and we did it. (I tried to always ask her and to respect the times she said no.) The day after the concert, I noted that "it was good to laugh and hear live music."

Me: "I have a haircut at 9 and am going to drop off some soda bread on my way from there to the Y."

S&R: "How about a movie and a bite to eat afterwards." A yes.

Me: "How about the Rose Garden at Elizabeth Park in Hartford for our promised holiday adventure?" A yes. Turned out that gorgeous weather made for an especially enjoyable day trip.

S: "Do you want to come over for hot dogs and corn on the cob to welcome in summer?" A yes.

S&R: "How about a light supper at Panera and ice cream at Brickley's?" A yes. Ice cream almost always sealed the deal for ME.

As the months passed, we got more invitations from them than we offered. I am grateful that equation never caused a schism in our friendship. Sandra and Roberta were our social circle. A shrinking world is not unusual in situations such as ours. It certainly adds to the stress of caregiving. And the toll it exacts is heavy.

Spring arrived early. That was good news because it made it easier for us to be out in the larger world, if only for shopping or drives. Any day that I was able to get ME out of the house was a good day. A really good day was one such as the Saturday we took advantage of *Smithsonian Magazine's* "Museum Day" to visit Slater Mill in Pawtucket. Although we lived just 38 miles away, we never had seen the historic textile mill and we never may have if I had not been constantly on the lookout for activities. Spring weather also allowed me to "escape" caregiving for a bit by working outside. I had daffodils to cut on March 19, perhaps the earliest date ever.

March also marked the completion of Luise's book, *Hope Healing Spirit /Strength, Solace and Self-Self-Advocacy for the Bipolar Community.* Her email after seeing it made my part in it worthwhile and was an important reminder to me of my value. It is, she wrote, "beyond my belief, beyond my ability to hold back tears, beyond my ability to do anything but to thank you, thank you, thank you." I answered that indeed her book was "something to celebrate. Quite an accomplishment. So cool to see. Glad you are HAPPY. I am, too."

I didn't tell her that I also was sad. That editing project — probably the most challenging of my career — had allowed me to get lost in work at the computer. It gave me permission to pay cursory attention to ME lurking in the doorway. It challenged me. It taught me. It rewarded me when I wrestled with awkward prose to finally find the word, phrase or sentence that conveyed meaning. It required me to be patient with someone else's unpredictable health, not just ME's, and doing so made me stronger. Perhaps most important, it reignited regular communication with my oldest friend.

What now? I wondered. The answer came within days. Another longtime friend, whose book I had edited, wrote with an inquiry from someone at her church who was in search of an editor. Within several days I had agreed to edit his manuscript for $150, with a turn-around time of about a month. I so wanted a project that I might have worked for nothing; given how the scope and time requirements of the project expanded, I practically did. In early April, however, I was just happy to have editing to look forward to.

I also was happy that my golf league would begin play in another month, but more than a bit apprehensive about that because I knew ME no longer could be left alone for an entire morning. I had two choices: Step away from golf or get help. Really, I had one choice, because there was no way I would give up golf. The game and the companionship of the women I played with were vital to my well-being. Help, which others had been urging for months (years), had to be arranged — and arranged quickly. I had read a newspaper story a year or more earlier about a new agency in town, HomeCare Assistance, and saved it (anticipating the inevitable, I suppose). I called on the sly and made an appointment, confident I could sneak way for an hour.

I arrived for that appointment nervous and unsure. I had prepared by searching online for advice about finding the right agency. I copied a list of questions to ask and pitfalls to watch out for. "Caregiving is not in my wheelhouse," I blurted out almost immediately. I wasn't proud of that, but there, I had said it. The director, Patricia, immediately put me at ease. I explained our situation and what I needed: someone Tuesdays 6 a.m. to noon. We talked about ME and me. I asked my questions; she gave me a folder of materials to read. It was reassuring to know that I could add hours if (when) needed. Although in the moment I could not imagine help beyond golf day, Patricia also said 24-7 coverage was possible, which could allow me to travel. I decided on the spot to go forward, and we agreed that Patricia would come to the house to meet ME.

I do not remember how I broke the news to ME. I do know that I did not ask her if this would be OK. I had waited too long to do that. I am pretty sure I focused on my uneasiness over leaving her alone while I played golf, and she maintained that she was capable of managing by herself. Whatever the nature of our conversation, I know ME was not happy with me. Thankfully, when Patricia came by on April 25 it went well, and ME seemed at least amenable to trying. Patricia also promised to return to introduce the "care assistant" on her first day. The stars must have aligned, because she actually brought Mary by a few days later to meet ME and chat. They hit it off from the get-go. ME offered our visitors tea, then took Mary to the kitchen with her. Shortly they were chatting and laughing. This might actually work, I thought, as I gave Patricia a thumbs-up.

After just a couple weeks, I wrote Luise that "ME loves the woman who comes Tuesdays 6-12. What a relief." She responded: "Big step; right step. . . . Enjoy the few hours you can call your own. I am very happy for you and ME." Luise was right on all counts. I had left the house the first morning with much trepidation, which Mary picked up on. She offered reassuring words before sending me off with a hug. Within a couple weeks, I was able to leave for the golf course feeling my load was lightened for at least a few hours. The consensus among family and friends seemed to be that this was a good first step, but help more frequently, even 24-7, would soon be necessary. As ME's cousin Jane put it, "You need to be on that page" and family members "will 100 percent support your decision."

Happily, we were off to Maine in mid-May, driving to Ogunquit one Tuesday after I finished golf and we ate lunch. As I wrote Luise, there were "moments of pleasure in being there. But [it was] also hard. ME not so good in confined space, i.e. the room. But [she] doesn't want to be outside either." Her frustration at times boiled over, and of course I was the "bad guy." I offered Jane another telling detail: ". . . it is clear that the change in locale increases her confusion and thus increases her dependence on me. And that is hard on me. It feels as if my independence has been taken away, too. And I have been nothing throughout my life but independent." Sigh

I had been stubborn, pushing us to do the trip in our "usual" way. It helped that we listened to an audio book on our three-hour drive, but what was I thinking when we chose *At the Water's Edge*, a complex story set in the Scottish Highlands during World War II? Did I really think three nights away from home would be a "vacation"? Was I delusional in hoping that ME would feel the familiar in places we had been visiting for decades?

Seldom did I leave Ogunquit (or, for that matter, any vacation spot) without wishing we could have stayed longer. ME never failed to remind me that it would be good to be home, that I should be satisfied with the time away we had. This trip was different because it had been difficult. It would take me a long time to realize that as troubled as I felt driving away from Sparhawk, that time with ME in our much-loved "beautiful place by the sea" had been a gift. Jane counseled afterward: "Forget the travel as a couple. It serves no good purpose. It confuses ME and puts you in a terrible bind. The only traveling I see is for you to get away from time to time. You need to."

Earlier Jane had characterized our situation in a way I had not, and which struck a chord: "It is an absolute tragedy what ME is going through, but what you are going through is worse. ME is in her world; you are trying to live in both worlds." Increasingly, her world was the one described by caregivers in their online posts and message boards. My world increasingly — disturbingly — included lurking on those sites more than I would like to admit. The proverbial moth drawn to a flame. I wanted to know if what I was experiencing was typical. I didn't want to know. I wanted to know what might lie ahead. I didn't want to know. I studied the stages of Alzheimer's to guess about where ME was. I didn't want to know.

As I explained to Jane, it was difficult "to watch/be part of the continuing cognitive decline. Of course, it is not linear. She will go days and days unsure about where to put trash, for just one example, and then for a day that is not an issue. ADLs generally confound her, and then not." I described going to a potluck birthday party for the 90-year-old husband of ME's longtime friend and research collaborator. It was important that we go, but for me it was a painful hour and a half because ME seemed so lost in a room full of people she had known her entire academic career.

As spring morphed into summer, I surreptitiously planned a week in Wisconsin with my family. A solo trip, as Jane had counseled. ME would have round-the-clock care assistants for a week in late July. I told her this; I did not ask her permission. She was more than a little upset about "people" being in the house. I was hopeful that having Mary for at least the first night would make things easier. I chuckle now when reading the lengthy notes I prepared for the care assistants, not unlike what new parents leave for a child's first babysitter. The night before I left, we had a light supper out with Roberta and Sandra, followed by ice cream. In advance, I had told them my approach was "not talking about the trip, in an attempt to lessen anxiety." Balancing my sensitivity to ME's moods (the disease), my attempts to avoid conflict and tamping down my growing anger was becoming a real struggle.

To avoid a scene the next morning, I had hoped to get out the door after Mary arrived and before ME came downstairs. No such luck. ME's hug was quick and perfunctory; she was not a happy camper. I really didn't care. It was not long before I wasn't a happy camper, either, when my flight out of Providence was delayed. I needed a stress-free trip, and it looked as if this would be anything but. Until the travel goddess intervened. I was at the airport early enough to get stand-by on a flight scheduled before mine. I made it, so I was in Milwaukee in time to be picked up by my nephew and his family driving from northern Virginia. Destination: Pelican Lake and a 100-year-old cabin that would be filled with family. The hot and humid weather traveled with me, but other than that it was the most wonderful, "normal" week I had experienced in a very long time. I even found consolation in knowing that had ME been able to be there, she would have hated most everything about the trip. Not surprisingly, after that respite I did not want to go home.

All the "good" of that week evaporated quickly when I returned. I tried to be grateful for my time away, but once I pulled into the driveway the weight of caregiving once more took over my life. Days later we found some relief from the oppressive heat inside our house when we joined Roberta and Sandra at their air-conditioned house for dinner before they left for a week on Cape Cod. In the decades of our friendship, there had been many years when we vacationed together, sometimes sharing a house, sometimes in our own rentals. How I envied their trip; how sad I was that ME and I could no longer share that. Even a day's visit was out of the question.

Enjoying AC after so many miserable days and especially nights at home (and in the Wisconsin cabin) prompted me to buy us a small window unit we could put in our den. The hell with anxiety over having it in a downstairs window at the front of the house. I found one at a big-box store, ordered it online, and we picked it up a couple hours later. Somehow we avoided a major meltdown while installing it. And that night we were able to watch Hillary Clinton's acceptance speech in relative comfort.

The evening provided me another period of profound sadness, however, as the historic moment was lost on ME. I was reminded of watching another such speech, with Luise, and emailed her: "Thought of you a lot last night . . . remembering us in Milwaukee watching McGovern. How the world has changed! It was sad, though, because ME really does not grasp much of all this. She spent her life working to advance women and is cheated out of this. I do plan to get her an absentee ballot to ensure she gets to cast her vote."

That email also included the news that I had arranged for ME to have additional care for four hours on Thursdays. It had gotten almost impossible to leave her alone for even a short time, and I needed a block of uncommitted freedom, not just to run errands but also to "catch my breath," to diffuse my anger. I hoped a little more time away from ME would help me be more patient, less emotionally distant, and able to continue our outings.

I believe it was sometime in mid-summer that I finally began to read *Into the Storm*. Barry Petersen's essay, "Lessons Learned," brought me up short and jolted me into action. Petersen, a CBS News correspondent, spoke to me in a way no one before or since has. His succinct broadcast prose got right to the heart of caregiving, and every one of his seven lessons resonated. I was immediately prompted to act on a legal matter I had avoided.

I had been unable to find the financial power of attorney that I was certain ME had signed when she updated her will and health-care power of attorney (I had them). I would need that if/when it became necessary to move ME. Unfortunately, ME's lawyer had died shortly after she signed those documents, and a search of her files was unsuccessful. I contacted my attorney for advice on my options. I was chagrined to learn that without that document, the only recourse was to seek guardianship. Yikes. I could not bear the thought of having to ask the court, in a public proceeding, to declare my partner "incompetent." I redoubled efforts to locate the POA. I snuck off to have lunch with Mike and Caryl in order to update them and seek their advice. They affirmed their full support of whatever I decided about guardianship and reiterated that my priority for ME's care should include taking care of myself.

I was not yet ready to be the priority, however, so I continued to deal with whatever a day brought with as much patience as I could muster. My head knew it was the disease causing behavior so unlike my gentle, quiet, caring partner. I didn't want to take it personally, but sometimes I couldn't help it. In those moments I didn't much like her and I didn't much like me. (The only place I found periodic emotional relief was in the shower, where I even occasionally allowed myself to cry.) Jane reassured me: "It has to be so hard dealing with things day to day and minute by minute. To say you seem to have adjusted well is an understatement."

So deal I did. I also:

- Finally conceded that, as I wrote Barbara in Georgia, "ME's memory issues make it impossible for her to make the trip to HHI any more. I refrained from ruling out this fall because I kept holding out hope it might work. But I need to be realistic and acknowledge that such travel would be hard for her and harder for me." I also acknowledged how much I needed "an island fix," and worked out dates for a spring visit with my sister.

- Got ME to Connecticut for a visit with family.

- Invited ME's friend Joan for an overnight visit to celebrate her birthday.

- Drove ME to church each week, often followed by a late breakfast at our favorite diner.

- Planned a trip for myself to Wisconsin.

- Continued work on the editing project as it dragged on.

In early September, I had to tell ME of the unexpected death of her goddaughter's husband, just 41. As difficult as getting her to the wake and funeral would be, among other reasons because an overnight motel stay would be involved, it was imperative that she be there. I saw to it that she was, remaining by her side the entire time.

Not long after, we did something rare: We had a house guest. My oldest nephew, then a Navy lieutenant commander, had a conference in Newport and asked to spend two nights before that with us. I was on tenterhooks the entire weekend, which proved to be 48 hours of "normalcy" — a gift for which I was immensely thankful. It was nice to have another adult in the house for conversation, especially one who loved ME and was accommodating to her. We took him out for seafood — followed by ice cream, of course. We had an educational visit to the Pequot Museum (with Dairy Queen on the way home), and drove around Newport before dropping him at his hotel.

I did not realize how much I missed conversation until I had it. I am not the most communicative person to begin with, but having the outlet taken away was frustrating. More often than not, I was reduced to saying yes or no to "sentences" that sadly made little or no sense. Early in the journey, I began taking a "20 Questions" approach with ME, but eventually even that no longer worked. As I told Jane, "I guess it is a pretty good thing that I am generally low maintenance. And I think it has finally sunk in that I cannot keep ME occupied during all waking hours."

By then, I had determined the time had come for additional hours of care assistance. But I knew those hours would be helpful only if I were out of the house because as long as I was there, ME now paid little attention to the care assistants — even our beloved Mary. I decided not to add hours at least until after my annual Sisters' Week in Wisconsin. What started out as an annual Packers-game weekend for Kris and me evolved after our retirements into a week together each fall. We even allowed my brother-in-law to join us for some activities, although we carved out lots of time just for the two of us.

ME's friend Joan said she would call daily, "unless you think that might upset the routine." I answered, "By all means, call." Jane also promised to call each day. And I knew Mike and Caryl would be in touch and likely visit. They all made leaving easier because, despite my eagerness to get away, I also felt a strong sense of responsibility for ME's well-being. (I continued to leave detailed instructions/notes for the care assistants.) The calls to ME were not easy, which Jane captured when she wrote me:

> The ME that we knew is no longer there. There were some moments that she connected but it was extremely limited. This is hard to say because when she talks her voice, her words, much of her affect is the same, so I am picturing the same person I [looked up to as a kid] but the thoughts and comprehension are not there. The world she is living in and relating to has little to do with her past.

And yet, when I look at a photo taken that week of ME and Mike on our screened porch, I see our ME. Ditto for the "cousins" photo from a month later, which we thankfully remembered to take just as Jane and her brother Bill were about to leave Connecticut after the visit we had finally engineered.

Perhaps that is why, despite all the evidence to the contrary, I went ahead with our fall trip to Maine. When I told Jane, she said I was "one brave woman to attempt it." She further wondered, "Will you be able to enjoy it?" It did not feel brave to me; it was what we had been doing for two or three days each October for almost thirty years. I was confident I could always enjoy Ogunquit; I only hoped the trip would bring ME some joy, too. Things went pretty well, but we did come home a day early. On Friday, we awoke to miserable weather that wasn't forecast to get better. There would be little chance to be outside or make the short walk to shop. And we certainly could not walk The Marginal Way along the Atlantic. In the "old days" we would have read and watched the storm. We would have donned raincoats and gone out to eat. But those days were long gone. I feared ME would not do well being cooped up in the room. I asked her if she wanted to head home in light of the weather and she immediately said yes. So we did. I knew it was for the best; I was not concerned that the room was unlikely to be re-booked for the night and some money would be lost. It never occurred to me that it would be our last trip to Ogunquit. Optimistic or delusional?

There was no doubting my state of mind the morning after Donald Trump was elected. ME and I had voted by absentee ballot. No way she could stand in line and go into the voting booth alone. No way I was going to allow her to miss the first opportunity to vote for a woman. The results came in long after we gave up watching TV coverage. I was up early the next morning, as usual, and the first thing I did was check online. I don't know that I ever have been as depressed as when I read the news. I could barely function all day. Luckily I had lunch planned with a friend, and it turned out we both needed to talk at length about the election. Sadly, ME's only reaction when I gave her the news was, "Oh." That only added to my sadness. The results so puzzled me that I immediately read *Hillbilly Elegy* in hopes of finding some understanding. Although it was a good read, it didn't get me there. Scary times ahead, I thought. But then, I was used to that; and what could be scarier than losing a loved one to dementia?

Thanksgiving buoyed my spirits, starting with an email from Luise to me and two other friends: "My life would be greatly diminished without the three of you holding me up. You are all high on my list of gratitude. Every Thanksgiving our family sits at the table and each person talks about the gratitude in their hearts. Each of you will be named. My heart swells with love for each of you." I responded to her the next day and caught her up on my life:

> Dear, dear friend — Thank you for this wonderful message. I read it at bedtime last night and it filled my heart. We were in Connecticut and had had a pretty good day, all things considered. But hearing from you made the day complete. We are back in RI now. After some downpours, it is almost springlike. I bought a pumpkin pie on the drive home and just got a pizza for dinner. I plan to hang out for the rest of the day.
>
> Life here is rather roller-coaster like, as is the nature of ME's disease. Thank goodness for a wonderful care assistant, Mary, whom ME adores. Still working to find a #2. So far two have not worked out. [I could have told her the tale of the one ME locked out of the house. I got the call just as I was leaving the golf course and rushed home to chaos. ME was, I think, put off by the young woman's age.] I have upped things to twice a week and am looking to three times a week starting in December. Sad that golf is over for a while, but I find that four hours goes pretty quickly.
>
> I am flying to D.C. on Tuesday, for two nights. Kris and Fred are there with their oldest and his family and a couple weeks ago when I was at a breaking point I invited myself down. Mary

could do the 24-7 so I was able to book the trip. Then in mid-January Kris, Fred and I are going to southern California to be with their youngest. They just had their second boy. Fred and I will stay a few days, then drive to Vegas together and leave from there. Kris will stay a couple weeks. See, I am trying to take care of myself.

I also shared what was weighing on my mind. I never was able to find the financial Power of Attorney, so I would have to go through the disquieting process of seeking guardianship. "That is just beginning and is going to be hard," I wrote. "But I know it has to be done, so . . . ."

December held little promise of "love and joy." Since both my parents died in December and ME's diagnosis in 2013 derailed our planned Christmas in Scotland, I have had no appetite for festivities. I tried to rekindle the spirit we had shared all those years of providing gifts for families in need. (My favorite story: Determined that a girl would get the "black Barbie" on her list, I took us to countless toy stores, until we had success in eastern Connecticut.) I had joined the "Shoebox" effort, but then was too sick with a cold to deliver them; ME and Mary got the pleasure. Kris had provided me with a three-foot Packers tree the year before, and I "decorated" that. I did a bit of shopping and committed to a short baking list.

Then in the middle of the month, I was felled by another monster cold. I barely slept. I had no care assistants booked. I finally reached out to Roberta and Sandra in hopes of getting cold medicine. "This came unexpectedly," I noted, "and has taught me to always have freezer food, cold cuts and prepared food in the pantry. Poor ME is not getting much nutrition." How did I not connect the dots from stress to my colds?

A week later, life was still a slog, but I was determined to make bourbon balls for my brother-in-law and get them in the mail. I did, but the effort finished me off for the day. Thank goodness for Hallmark-channel movies, "Gilmore Girls" binging and a recliner for napping. Thank goodness for the day when I had Mary for a few hours and I could wearily run errands. "I have conceded that holiday baking is not happening this year," I told Sandra. That meant Mike would have to make do without his mother's tea cookies. Sadly, ME could not make them for him anymore. Sadly, she didn't remember making them.

I had not expected much Christmas-day merrymaking, and the morning was indeed difficult — at least for me. ME really did not seem to "get it." Opening gifts was a challenge for her, and it saddened me to watch her almost total lack of affect. As for me, I tried my best to get past the reality of receiving no gifts from her. (The previous Christmas she gave me a $100 bill, tucked in a card, like she gave her nieces and nephews.) Once, Christmas in our home was quite the festive production, but no more.

We were able to drive to Connecticut mid-afternoon, however, and things there went pretty well. ME loved being around the younger "grands," and her nieces and nephews were patient and loving with her. We missed that she no longer could be the designated gravy maker. We chuckled at how she still insisted on cleaning the sink. The chaotic gift opening again was confusing for her. I was glad we had chosen to spend the night because the day was long.

Amazing how the holiday rushes by and suddenly it is December 26 — just another day. We got home about noon. For the first few minutes of the drive, ME had been more "talkative" than she had been in a long time. I took that as a good sign. But then once home, where I gave in to fatigue, she once again was enveloped by confusion. Such is the nature of the disease for her. When her Massachusetts brother called to ask about visiting the next day, I suggested the weekend instead. I was proud of myself for that. I didn't tell him it was because I was worn out, had a care assistant coming, and very much needed a few hours for myself. Such is the nature of caregiving.

Little did I know we had just enjoyed our last Christmas at home. Little did I know that the new year would be one of change, change, change.

"As I grew older, I realized how little control we really have over what we are given in this world. And I no longer battled with my demons. I just grew to accept that they were a part of me. Like an ache in my bones that I try to shake every day that I awaken, an internal fight within myself not to look back, but to focus on each new day."

The Lost Wife
Alyson Richman

CHAPTER 6

No Escaping Reality

June 26, 2017, was beautiful in southern Rhode Island. At 9:15 a.m. I walked ME out to my car. She wore black capris, a striped LL Bean cotton blouse over a purple-striped golf shirt, black crew socks and her scuffed New Balance sneakers. She carried her two "babies" and her large, purple Vera Bradley purse; inside she had doll clothes. I knew what she could not: It was the last time she would leave our house. I swallowed hard to keep my emotions in check. I had to hold it together until after I walked out of Wellspring Village, the memory-care unit of a continuous-care community where she would live.

There was no "straw that broke the camel's back" and brought us to that moment. A more apt description is a bale of straw coming apart until the whole of it lay scattered about, trampled on. The chaos of the first six months of the new year led inexorably to the decision I had resisted making until I had no choice. I found no solace in Barry Petersen's observation that "almost no one gets this [decision] right."

The year had begun with me looking forward to a short, mid-January trip to California with my sister and brother-in-law. Care assistants now were a way of life, and I had grown used to — if not yet entirely comfortable with — the idea of making more time for myself. I also had grown used to being "flat out" day after day, from early morning until late evening. January 12 handed me what I described as "the sad but true story of my $600 day-trip to Chicago Midway." It is worth recounting in detail because it reflects what I was willing to put up with just to get away.

My day started with the dreaded 5:45 a.m. flight — requiring me to get up at 3. I had slept (poorly) on the couch so as not to disturb ME and care assistant Mary, who spent the night. My plan was to fly to Las Vegas, through Midway; meet Kris and Fred; drive four hours to Ridgecrest, where my youngest nephew and family were stationed. At some point at the Providence airport, I got a text saying weather might impact my flight and offering me a chance to change it. But because they already were going to be waiting more than two hours for me in Vegas, I decided to take my chances and stick with my original itinerary. I gambled and lost!

The flight from Providence was uneventful and I dozed most of the way. As luck would have it, though, there was a thin band of nasty "icy mix" moving through Chicago about the same time as my flight, which caused some turbulence. Landing at Midway is a challenge in the best of weather; our pilots nailed it, despite slick conditions and having circled for about 45 minutes. I made my way to an information board and saw that my next flight had been cancelled, as had most others to Vegas. So I joined the line at the gate. Two and a half hours later (having had no coffee and only a Clif bar), I was not surprised to learn that the earliest I could get there was Friday night. I already had decided that my Plan B would be to return to Providence. My trip was a short one to begin with, and I could not ask my family to wait a day and a half for me. I secured a seat on an afternoon flight. I texted Kris, who was still en route. I texted Mary. I called the agency to cancel the care assistants I had booked. I texted Mike and Caryl. And I tried to keep from crying. I did manage to enjoy a leisurely early lunch at a favorite eatery and a bag of caramel-cheese-mix popcorn.

Fast forward to Providence, after another uneventful flight, including another vacant middle seat. I hoofed it to Baggage Service, because my lucky luggage *did* go to Vegas. A very nice woman got my whole sad story; in my exhaustion I was more talkative than usual. She filled out a report, offered me a $100 voucher for my inconvenience, and wished me the best. Tired, bummed out and depressed, I finally arrived home about 6. Mary, angel that she was, stayed to make my supper and clean up. Come Saturday morning, I still was waiting for my luggage, so I made the best of it by cleaning out the bathroom closet and drawers that had been driving me wacky for months. My bag finally was delivered Saturday night. During my Friday-night ruminating, it had occurred to me that the Vegas-to-home leg of my trip was still active. I promptly cancelled it for a credit — thereby it had actually been just a $300 day trip. Somehow I was able to find that bit of humor in my traveler's nightmare. Incredible, because humor had been in short supply lately. It was about to get worse. And my bad travel karma was just getting started.

I had dragged my feet about pursuing guardianship after I learned the legal notice had to be published in the local newspaper. Ever protective of ME's privacy, I dreaded the thought that someone who knew her would see it. I continued to believe that if only I looked in the right spot, I would find the financial POA. After all, ME saved *everything*. By late January, however, I had no choice but to begin the guardianship petition. About the same time, I arranged to add more care-assistant hours beginning February 1: Mondays, Tuesdays, Thursdays and Fridays 9-2. I can manage with that, I thought. There would be some continuity in help for ME and relief for me. Enough relief that I could make it from Friday afternoon to Monday morning. Hah!

There was no escaping the brutal realities of Alzheimer's. Although the disease does not manifest the same way in everyone, I knew from the medical folks and my reading what I might expect. I had dealt with or was about to deal with many — but not all — of these: agitation, anger, paranoia, personal hygiene issues, hallucinations, sleep issues, aggression, depression, appetite changes, mood swings, wandering, hoarding, incontinence, delusions, confusion, inability to follow directions, repetitive speech, repetitive behaviors.

I have lengthy notes recording my experiences in excruciating detail. At first it was me writing for me as I accounted for the causes of my frustration, fatigue, anger and hurt. Eventually I wrote notes to share privately with Mary, to fill in the gaps between her care assistance and my caregiving. Sometimes I would vent with family members or confide in the friends who were my support system. Anything to validate what I knew to be true: It was the disease, not ME — who, truth be told, I didn't much like anymore. Jane's understanding was the gift that kept on giving, as she reassured me: "I know what you mean about there being no love. The person who you did love is no longer alive. ME stopped existing months and months ago. You are now basically living with a stranger who is taking all your energy and sanity away."

I continued to see getting away as the answer. A friend and I had been talking for months about a short "travel adventure." We finally booked a getaway to The Litchfield Inn, in the snow-belt hills of western Connecticut. We knew early February travel in New England was problematic, but the inn's cancellation policy convinced us to book our rooms. I opted for one of the slightly pricier theme rooms, unable to resist the funky Bohemian Room.

On the morning we were to leave, icy rain delayed us a couple hours. The forecast was promising, though, and once Linda arrived from Providence we quickly packed my car and headed off on our 2 1/2 hour drive. The roads were messy, but we eventually made it to the inn. (Was the sheet-of-ice parking area an omen?) After settling into our rooms, we agreed to meet in a couple hours for a "dinner" of wine, cheese, sausage, crackers and chocolates in front of the fireplace in my room.

I went to the workout room to ride the recumbent bike, then checked the news. The forecast for the day of our return suddenly included snow — perhaps a lot of it. That unsettled us enough to ask about our options should we leave early, but we agreed to wait until morning to plan. By breakfast, it seemed we might get stuck in Litchfield for an extra night. Drat! Reluctantly, we decided it would be prudent to return to Rhode Island. Amazingly, we enjoyed a sunny, scenic drive that prompted us to stop for a leisurely lunch at the Saybrook Point Resort, nestled between Long Island Sound and the Connecticut River. Linda eventually got to Providence; I got back to caregiving.

I also returned to dealing with guardianship. My lawyer had counseled me that the process would take some time, so it was better to "have it settled before you need it." As it turned out, it would take even longer than expected — and I already needed it. If only I had read Barry Petersen's essay earlier, because he was so correct when he wrote that "when, not if, [caregiving] reaches the point that it is overwhelming . . . for the caregiver, you waited too long."

About this time, ME and I saw what turned out to be our last movie together in a theater. I had chosen "LaLa Land" because I thought the singing and dancing would hold her attention, with little need to follow a plot. I was wrong. She was restless; ten minutes in, she asked, "So do you want to go?" Throughout the movie, she frequently talked aloud to me (ironic because such talking bothered her so much that we always tried to sit in the last row, or away from other patrons). Somehow we made it to the end of the movie. She was happy to walk out; I was profoundly sad. The ever-changeable disease had won again. Our world continued to shrink.

I noticed that she was having more difficult days than not, although it was unpredictable and so each day was an adventure. After a dental appointment, I took her and Mary to lunch at a local diner. ME saw a couple of people she recognized and her face lit up. That was nice to see. One Monday in late March, she "had the best day I can remember in perhaps a year or more. This after a horrible Friday," I wrote in a note. Tuesday, however, "was again terrible."

There continued to be some respite in taking drives, especially when they included ice cream or Dairy Queen. We both grew up with fathers who enjoyed driving a route over and over, so our outings seldom were a hardship. I learned that the Fifties station on Sirius was soothing; my favorite Sixties music not so much. (To this day I switch to the Fifties on the weekends!) I can chuckle about it now, but one of those drives scared the bejesus out of me. ME had been more confused than usual, so after lunch I decided an outing might help. I stopped for gas and briefly turned away from the car, toward the pump. When I finished and opened my car door, I saw the other seat was empty. How did she get out; the seatbelt had baffled her for weeks? I looked around. Nothing. Where could she have gone, I frantically wondered. Finally I found her inside the station. "I came in to look for you," she rather calmly explained. "Please don't ever do that again," I begged, momentarily overlooking the fact that I might as well be talking gibberish.

Not long after, in early April, we had a Friday night that was not my finest hour. Suffice it to say that I foolishly tried to reason with ME — at midnight — then yelled and ordered her to get into bed. I broke every "rule" I had learned about communicating with a person with Alzheimer's. In the moment, all I could feel was my own exhaustion. In the quiet of the next morning, I was sad. I also was beginning to realize that even the additional hours of caregiving help were not enough. A two-night return — by myself — to the Litchfield Inn and the Bohemian Room allowed me to decompress a bit, I told Jane, "and begin to relearn being on my own." She had asked me awhile back if I had given any thought to how I saw my future, "and I actually spent some time thinking on that," I told her, but "NO answers — yet." I added that I was trying to plan some time away every month, including ten days in Virginia. "I do worry that that much time away will be difficult on ME, but it has to be," I added.

Miraculously, my notes describe a stretch of "good" days shortly after my Friday night meltdown. Ah, the roller coaster ride that is Alzheimer's!

During that stretch, ME did something she had resisted for days and days, so I complimented her profusely in hopes of reinforcing the behavior. She was generally calm and cooperative. She enjoyed watching old TV shows and the Red Sox. We ventured out to lunch at a familiar hometown restaurant, then stopped for ice cream. A couple days later we tried a tony Watch Hill spot for lunch. Bad choice; service was slow and it was noisy. ME agreed when I suggested not going there again. One afternoon, after a "lunch" of Dairy Queen, ME sat on the couch with me as I sorted a box of photographs from her mother's house. She chuckled at some of them, but was not able to identify many of the people. I set most aside to give to Mike. I did not want to be the one to toss them.

April 16 was Easter. It felt strange to not have ME going off to church but instead watching "Curious George" after drinking her morning tea (she long ago had abandoned coffee for Irish tea). It felt strange to not have even a little Easter basket, we who had packed candy, "grass" and baskets for an Easter spent at a Women's Final Four basketball tournament. At least we had dinner with the family in Connecticut to look forward to. The two-hour drive was uneventful, but ME was ready to return home after a couple of hours. I think the noise and chaos of family gatherings had become too much for her. We left shortly after eating; the ride home was very quiet. The next morning I was reading about "sundowning" on the ALZ discussion board when ME came downstairs. I wish I had known earlier that fatigue can be a trigger, as can the stress of activity.

I found myself looking at that discussion board more and more often, searching for posts on a behavior, a medication or some such. To an extent, the posts proved reassuring, and it could be helpful to see what others in my situation had to say. But at times the posts also reinforced my skepticism about groups, where generalizing and ill-informed opinions annoy me. I needed information, but wanted it on my stubborn terms.

I had no qualms about the agency I had turned to or the care assistants it was able to provide. As I added hours, and as I traveled more often, ME had to get used to new women. She resisted, and took to some more than others, but with two exceptions they worked out, for which I am eternally grateful. Overnights were challenging, but when Mary could provide coverage things usually went well. In mid-April, however, her own mother's illness and subsequent death kept her out of the rotation for a while. Coincidentally, I was going to Virginia. Bless her heart, Mary arrived for the first night of my absence. We did not know until then that her mother's funeral had been the day before. She had a cold and was exhausted, but told me there was no way that she wanted to abandon us. ME was so happy to see her — content to sit with her on the couch as we talked. They went upstairs about 9, because I had another early flight and was going to sleep downstairs. I got ME to give me a hug, but realized she did not seem to understand that I was leaving. Probably for the best, I thought to myself.

For once, my travel was without problems; the flight to National Airport even landed early. This trip promised pomp, as we would gather for my nephew's retirement ceremony after twenty-plus years in Naval aviation, and fun in the trip my sister and I then would make to Hilton Head. It was incredible to return to the Pentagon; my first visit the previous November had been an unexpected treat. My heart was full as we tucked ourselves into a conference room for the formalities (so different from my retirement experience, and he so young!). It seemed not that long ago I had been at his high school graduation, then Annapolis for his USNA graduation. I was touched when Bill had a rose for his wife, his mother — and me. I was touched when he said loving things about me in his remarks. I barely held it together when he handed me one of his ceremonial challenge coins. And when my brother-in-law pressed into my hand the challenge coin from the USS Green Bay he had just been given by a colleague of Bill's, I had all I could do to keep from sobbing.

Lunch was at an Afghani restaurant, and I was proud of myself for uncharacteristically sampling everything on the buffet. Back at the house, we got into comfy clothes, talked of the day and Bill's career, migrated outdoors into the beautiful spring afternoon. My youngest grand-nephew wanted to blow bubbles. I joined him. His laughter and joy added years to my life. So did adult conversation that stretched late into the evening. I finally went to bed about 11, unable to remember when I last had been up so late. Luckily, our next-day flight was not until noon.

We flew direct from Dulles to Savannah. It was a smallish, regional jet, but I long ago had gotten comfortable with them. And given the current circumstances of my life, I would have endured a bus ride if it got me to Hilton Head. For once, we had a rental car that was *not* white — it was red, yay! — which seemed a good omen. At the house, while unpacking, I said to Kris: "I don't know how to feel" about being there without ME for the first time. She advised me to "take a deep breath and move forward." Looking back, I see her advice was a true gift. I moved forward — with baby steps — many times on that trip.

We went for dinner at a restaurant ME and I loved, and I was prepared to order my favorite meal, ribs. But at the last minute I decided I did not want to do what I always had done, so I ordered shrimp skewers. I carried that attitude with me throughout the week. We lived on the sun porch, never once using the living room and seldom turning on the television. We saw that replicas of the Niña and Pinta were in Beaufort, so decided to tour them and enjoy the town. (We got stuck in traffic on the drawbridge; it was nice not to be in a hurry.) We shopped, Kris admittedly much more than I. We felt so "with it" when we found "spinners" for her grandsons, each of us having learned about the "hot toy" in different ways just that morning. I ate my fill of shrimp. We tried a new-to-us pizza place instead of the one ME and I had gone to forever. Serendipity found us on a water taxi to Daufuskie Island, a place I had long wanted to visit. It was a perfect day to be on the water. It was a perfect day for exploring by golf cart. The island is a step back in time, for sure, and we explored its historic sites and tiny museum. It was a perfect day for lunch and conversation with strangers at a communal table at Lucy Bell's, where I had my first shrimp tacos. One evening we agreed that if we were up in time the next day, we would go to the beach to watch the 6:40 sunrise. I awoke at 6:38 and bagged it. I could do that; I was "free."

Amazingly, I resisted calling home to check on ME; it felt better to let the care assistant handling the weekend manage things. When I knew Mary was back on duty, I texted her and she said things were unsettled. I did not sleep well. The following day she had better news. "Enjoy yourself," she said. Instant relief for me. ME moved to the back of my mind — until the day before we left. I remembered I wanted to bring her slices of the Key lime poundcake she always had enjoyed. I was sad about leaving Hilton Head and apprehensive about what I was going home to. I tossed and turned all night.

Two uneventful flights brought me to Providence. My luggage arrived quickly, and it was not long before I had retrieved my car and was on my way home — with trepidation. It was 80 degrees when I pulled into the driveway. I had not even gotten out of the car when I was greeted by ME — in her nightclothes. When I left, she liked Kathy, the overnight care assistant. Not anymore. Kathy signed out quickly. After less than ten minutes home, I was frustrated and on the verge of tears. Sadness followed, including when the poundcake was ignored.

My notes for the rest of April and May document a steady slide, as Alzheimer's continued its assault on ME and me. There were periods of calm. There even were moments when ME was "playful," laughed at TV shows, dried a dish or two on her own. But such moments were rare, and the periods of calm were shorter and shorter. I was in contact with CR, her nurse practitioner — on the sly, phone calls from the car when ME was with a care assistant. Meds were adjusted. Meds were changed. ME's appointments with her had become more frequent, and for the most part she still responded to CR. But I could see that relationship was going south, too. CR remained a significant support for me, but there was no longer much she could do for ME.

As far back as January, ME had begun complaining about back and leg pain. Her doctor suggested it might be sciatica, so we treated it as such. The heating pad became her best friend. But her inability to describe her pain made helping her difficult. I could see her wince, walk gingerly. It did not help that she had begun to go up and down the stairs dozens of times each day. Often I found myself walking behind her, ready if she should begin to falter or fall. That behavior got old quickly and remained a source of irritation, especially as the weather got warmer and the upstairs hotter.

About this same time, the starts and stops of the guardianship process got worked out. Her brothers wrote their letters supporting my petition. The required paperwork attesting to her "incompetency" was secured. Mike was there for me every step of the way. I can't count the number of times I called him — from the car, of course — with a question, with a rant, with a request, with an unspoken cry to have someone listen. One final hiccup would be my fault. I wondered — a week before the hearing — if it would be best for ME to be in Connecticut, where she had so many people who loved her. Part of me was thinking that would let me off the hook of continued responsibility for her. Ultimately, however, I knew that was not the right decision, that she was my partner and I would not let her down. I *was* her guardian and always should be. And down the road, when the time came, I wanted her close to me.

The law required that the guardianship notice be read to ME. I dreaded that. The constable's visit was scheduled for the afternoon of Friday, May 26. As could only happen in a community as small as ours, it turned out we had worked with his wife at the university! The reading did not take long. ME was briefly agitated by something he said, then sat down, the blank look of dementia on her face. When he finished, he handed her the papers. She handed them to me. And that was that.

Next up: a visit from the Guardian ad Litem, who would make a recommendation on my petition to the Probate judge. He also would gather information such as personal history, information on assets and how her day-to-day needs were being met. I don't remember a lot about his visit, except that I was uncomfortable. The attorney was personable, professional, kind. It seemed immediately obvious to me — and I believe to him — why guardianship was required, and there was nothing to suggest I was not the right person. In short order, my lawyer was ready to file the petition. It was too late for March and, as luck would have it, I had out-of-town reservations for both the April and May court dates. So I ended up on the Probate Court docket for June 22.

In the meantime, the care assistants and I did our best. They had the distinct advantage of short shifts, although most days I imagine those shifts *felt* never ending. For the remaining 18 or 20 hours, it was ME and me. Barb trying her best. Barb still trying to reason, even though she knew that was hopeless. Barb still struggling to make social outings happen. Barb pained when yet again ME was uncomfortable, unresponsive, blank. Barb trying to put healthy meals on the table, to fix the foods ME enjoyed — or at least *used to enjoy.* Barb battling her own discomfort with someone else's ADLs. Barb discovering a "trick" that worked and had a desired outcome, and then the next time, or time after that, did not. Barb trying not to yell back in frustration, too tired sometimes to care that she had. Barb wondering how much yelling, begging, cajoling the neighbors heard through open windows. But only once did I give up and retreat to the guest room! And that lasted only a couple of hours and provided no sleep.

Barry Petersen's sixth lesson — "Caregivers are people until they stop being people" — became real to me, but only in retrospect. It is that point, he explained, at which one realizes "the demands on you increase, but the appreciation from the person can disappear." I felt that lack of appreciation deeply, took it personally when it was not. At the same time, my notes reveal to me, I would not allow myself to "give up" on ME.

She had designed our house (pre-us) so the downstairs room we used as a den was a "legal" bedroom. She had done that in anticipation of her mother someday needing to live with her. I think she also believed that were one of us to require care at home, the room could easily be repurposed. I, on the other hand, could never imagine her ill mother (or mine, for that matter) living with us. Nor could I imagine any scenario where I was the caregiver of ME confined to that room.

As much as I knew that ME wanted to remain at home regardless of the circumstances, I could imagine that *not* being possible. I cringed at the commercials where a family member promises to keep another family member at home. The longer I was a caregiver, the more deeply offended I was. How dare "they" imply that this is the high ground? What happens if you cannot? The promise I had made to ME — shortly after her diagnosis and at critical times after that — was that I would always make sure she was cared for. I did not promise that care would always be at home. I did not promise that I would always be the one providing that care.

On ME's birthday, May 30, I wrote my friend Luise: "I understand that it is the disease, not her, but I have reached the limit of what I am willing to take. . . . A sentence I saw recently said that their happiness is not the goal, keeping them safe and well cared for is. I am trying to figure out how to keep that happening without me doing it."

In early June, I was ready to let go of caregiving — I just had not verbalized it yet. On the 8th, I took ME for an appointment with her nurse practitioner. It did not go well. She did not seem to remember she had been seeing CR regularly for four years. She told her that she was fine and not having any problems. It got so nasty when CR asked me questions — with ME's permission — that we quickly agreed to talk later by phone to decide a course of action.

By the middle of June I finally acknowledged that I had reached my breaking point. "It is the last time I am going to do this," I wrote in a note to Mary after another battle over an ADL. I contacted Mike and said it was time for memory care, and I thought the Hamden area would be best because there were potentially more people to visit ME. I asked him to scout possibilities and told him I would call a place in town that seemed promising. "It has to happen sooner rather than later," I wrote to Jane, who had perceived the need long before I did.

My situation had changed, and so had I. I was emotionally black and blue. Thankfully, I had returned to therapy on May 25. I had left my first voicemail inquiry with Beverly, jumbled I am sure, a week or so before that. I was desperate and frantic when I made that call from the Narragansett Beach parking lot. I later learned that my very first session with her in 1990 had been within a day or two of that date! I marveled at the serendipity of that.

As I counted down the days to the guardianship hearing, I spent the weekend before in Northampton, Massachusetts, where my nephew Bill was participating in the Django in June "guitar camp." While he took classes, I enjoyed my splurge at the historic (and outrageously expensive) Hotel Northampton. I also explored the Emily Dickinson Museum in nearby Amherst, which ME and I always intended to do. Bill and I drove back to Rhode Island on Father's Day after a delightful weekend of Gypsy jazz, conversation and food — and for me a modicum of peace. Not so at home. My world had been spinning out of control for so long. Now, with my decision to move ME to memory care as soon after the guardianship hearings as possible, things moved at the speed of light.

Monday, June 19 — I had an 11 a.m. appointment about memory care at WV, just a few miles from home. I was nervous on the drive over, more nervous upon arrival. I was happy that after initially saying no, I accepted my friend Libby's offer to go with me. A second set of ears proved invaluable, but equally important was her moral support. I was bowled over by the facility; so was she. Darlene, executive director of the senior-living complex, was friendly, kind, knowledgeable, understanding, patient. She put me/us at ease. Thankfully, an apartment was immediately available. When we left about 12:15 p.m., I had set in motion a plan to move ME there by the 26th. By the way, I had gone there with no Plan B.

I immediately emailed Patricia at the home-care agency to let her know what I was doing and to adjust my schedule. I was effusive in my praise: "Without your guidance and the loving care offered by all those caring for ME, especially Mary, I would not have been able to keep ME at home as long as this. I learned so much from all of you. And I will be forever grateful."

Tuesday, June 20 — It was a damp and foggy golf morning. Libby and I were in charge of checking in players, so we were at the course early. She suggested that instead of playing, we go furniture shopping for ME's apartment, which was on my agenda for later in the day. First we had breakfast on the way to her house, where I finished the paperwork I had begun surreptitiously the night before. We both hate to shop, but within 90 minutes of arriving at the furniture store we had chosen a bed, dresser, nightstand, mattress set and recliner — for delivery on Friday! My list still included a hallway table, lamps and other things, but this seemed like amazing progress. I got Libby home, grabbed a bite of lunch and headed to Providence for a therapy session. What great timing. It helped me to talk freely about what was transpiring, to hear Beverly's affirmation of my actions and thoughts.

Back home, Mary was distraught; her shift had been, she said, "the longest 12 hours ever." I could see how difficult it was for her. We both knew it was her last time with ME but could not show it. It broke my heart to think about how ME — or, rather, ME's disease — had been treating her lately. How things had changed since Mary first came into our lives 14 months earlier. That I developed into the caregiver I was, that I hung on as long as I did, was in large measure because of the caregiver Mary modeled. As she drove away, after a long hug at the front door, I could see she was crying. I fought my own tears, then returned to the painful chore of caregiving.

Wednesday, June 21 — At 9:30, the nursing director (H) and memory-care-unit director (J) arrived to do their assessment of ME. They saw her at her worst, which disturbed me but probably was a good thing. We got through it, me providing the information they needed to plan for her care. ME seemed comfortable with J when they walked away to chat a bit. There was "nothing good about the rest of the day," I wrote in a note.

Thursday, June 22 — The date I had anticipated and dreaded. I had a full day: more shopping for the apartment, Weight Watchers at noon, guardianship hearing at 2. I had not been sleeping well — or long. I was apprehensive about the hearing. (I think the only time I had been in front of a judge was for my brother's adoption back in the Fifties.) The courtroom was stifling. The hearing itself was pretty much a non-event, considering the worry and stress that preceded it. After just a couple minutes, I walked out of the room as the legal guardian of ME, person and estate.

Friday, June 23 — I had booked a care assistant for 9 because I had a 9:30 appointment to sign the lease for ME's apartment. While waiting in the lobby, I had a wonderful chat with a staff member. Once more I felt extremely fortunate to have found care for ME so close to home. (I wondered in a note to myself whether I now needed to put *home* inside quotation marks.) After the paperwork was taken care of, I emptied my car of supplies, clothing and a few personal items for the apartment (actually one big room with ensuite bath), then set off in search of a hallway table. Surprisingly I found one at my first stop, drove it back to the apartment, ran a few errands, grabbed a salad at McDonald's and made it home in time for the care assistant's shift to end at 1. Whew. Then about 3 I got a call from J; the furniture was delivered but the bed appeared to be too high. Oh my. It took some doing, but I arranged to have the box spring swapped out, which could be done on Sunday.

Saturday, June 24 — No surprise, but I had slept especially poorly and was downstairs by 4:30 and semi-awake long before then. I knew I was hanging on by a thread. In my note, I wrote: "I know the stress is bad for me, and the sitting. I have not been able to make time for the Y. That is about to change, as long as I can hold on." My uneasiness about performing personal care had begun to play out in ways that I was not comfortable with. It seemed eons ago that I did not see myself as a caregiver because that profile did not fit me. I could hold on for one final weekend.

It wasn't easy. In order to get ME's apartment set up, I had booked a care assistant for four hours on Sunday. There was an unsettled period on Saturday as the agency director and I negotiated who that could be. ME was up earlier than usual. I had made plans for us to meet Mike and Caryl for lunch. ME was uncooperative, said she wasn't going because she wasn't invited. I reluctantly cancelled. Eventually I got us out for a short drive, to buy fresh strawberries. At home I withdrew into silence. By 5 there was not yet resolution of Sunday's caregiving. I was frantic. I did not know what I would do if I did not get that help. Finally Patricia texted to say she would take the shift 11-3. I was saved. ME and I spent a quiet evening watching the Red Sox.

Sunday, June 25 — My note for the day was simple: "I have been awake since 3:30, up since 4:30. I am not going to try to capture all that swirls within me, that can wait for later. But I have concluded that when I strip everything away, what is here is overwhelming sorrow." Jane wrote to offer support. "Today will be hard. Anticipating the relief of tomorrow will probably make today seem 100 hours long."

I remember Patricia's calming presence, her ability to soothe ME. I remember four hectic hours of work to make ME's new space cozy and at least a little bit familiar for her. I remember returning home to Mike and Caryl's surprise visit. (If they arrived with any doubts about the imminent move, they surely left without them.) I remember walking Patricia to her car and being comforted by her reassuring words and a hug. I don't remember anything else about that day, nor can I find any notes. Probably that is just as well.

Monday, June 26 — I had known for some time that my responsibility to ME was to ensure that she was safe and well cared for. Like so many caregivers, I finally had concluded that no longer was possible at home. I was luckier than many; no family drama caused consternation about my decision. Indeed, family and friends alike had seen the need for this day *long* before I was able to acknowledge it. Nonetheless, I awoke knowing there would be nothing easy about it.

As usual, my day started early. As I greeted the world, I asked for strength and courage and expressed gratitude. Then I opened my iPad to a message from my brother-in-law, which offered all of those. It had me in tears, as it does every time I read it. Later I learned that he purposely timed its sending so I would not see it until the morning.

> We plan on talking to you tomorrow night to make sure you're ok, but I wanted to talk to you right now as well. Barb, you have done a very difficult task magnificently for all of the years since ME's illness began. You told us maybe 2 years ago that you were never cut out to be a caregiver, but you were so very wrong. You're a very strong woman, Barb, and I, for one, am humbled by you. I hope that I will be as strong as you are if I'm ever faced with a similar situation. That having been said, I'd like to ask you a favor. Please remember the moment I shook your hand at the Pentagon, and passed the USS Green Bay challenge coin to you. Take that moment with you tomorrow, and know that your hand is firmly in mine, and that Kris and I are here for you after your difficult job tomorrow, and for all time after that. You are never alone, Barb, and I'm positive I speak for our whole family. We ALL love you, Barb, and we want to be there for you.

ME was up at 6:15 — incredibly early for her. I wonder even today if she sensed something was afoot. She was generally calm and cooperative. I tried to tame her hair, without success. I felt a failure for being unable to succeed at personal care. "I know my limits, and they have been to her detriment," I wrote, adding that "I amazed myself" with the help I *had* been able to provide. "Had she not reached a place in her disease where she no longer would let care assistants help with those things, perhaps she could still be at home. Sadly, that was not the course her dementia chose." I suspect that sooner or later, all dementia follows that course.

I snuck around the house gathering a few more things to personalize her apartment. It is funny how easily I could be sneaky and come up with "fiblets" (aka therapeutic lies). In passing, I told her I was getting things ready because she was going to get some rehab for her leg and ankle, and that she would have to stay there so her insurance would pay for it. Rehab wanted her to use her own pillows, I said, so I put her favorite purple pillowcases on them.

Our arrival at WV went well, except for when the receptionist asked, "ME is the one moving in?" ME asked, "Moving in?" And I quickly responded, "Moving in for rehab." The nurse walked her off to get coffee so I could put things in her room. After I met the aide who would help with her personal care, I went with J to check on the new box springs. From the hall, I could see ME and the nurse heading toward the outdoor courtyard. It seemed like a good time for me to leave. And so I did.

"I found myself wondering whether a shared memory can exist if one of the people sharing it no longer remembers it."

Susan Orlean
The Library Book

CHAPTER 7

Memory Care

I hate roller coasters — the steep ups, sharp curves and steeper downs, the total lack of control. More accurately, I hate the idea of roller coasters, because I never have ridden one. But it is my best metaphor for my life AD. I know for certain that I expected to be able to describe things differently after ME moved into memory care. While I did not expect the roller coaster rides to end immediately, I expected them to end. They did not. Barry Petersen's first lesson — "You will never get ahead of this changing disease" — took on new meaning for me.

As I was leaving WV on June 26, Darlene came out of her office to ask how I was doing. She noted that a social worker was available. I said thanks, but I have a therapist. "Don't hesitate to use us if you want to double-up," she answered. "We are here for you, too." I asked her how soon I "should" visit ME. She advised, "Follow your heart." At that moment, my heart wanted to be anywhere else for some time.

I drove home. Numb. Beaten down. Exhausted. In a fog. I curled up on our/my bed, but only a few tears would come. It felt as if there should be a lot more. I cursed the cruelty of dementia, the unfairness of it. Then I changed the sheets, because I did not want to face that later. I took the over-sized purple blanket and threw it on the floor in the guest room. "I never want to use you again," I yelled. I did not want to be reminded of ME's compulsive straightening of it over and over every night and throughout the day. The blanket also reminded me of the depth of my frustration and how often I had let that get the better of me.

I had been afraid of ME overhearing a mention of my plan, so Libby was the only friend who knew about the move in advance. She had invited me to go to lunch afterward, and when I felt ready I drove to Great Island. She, John and I sat inside because it was too breezy to be on the porch. As I looked out at the water, I recounted the morning in excruciating detail. Bless them for listening. I choked up at times, but mostly held my tears in check. Why has doing so always been so important for me? If ever I had a reason to cry with friends, wasn't this it? Later, Libby and I were able to enjoy our Weight Watchers-friendly lobster salads outdoors at a nearby restaurant. There were moments, such as when I snapped a photo to text to my lobster-loving sister, where I felt "normal." Eventually, though, it was time for me to return to my empty house. Nothing at all normal about that.

My afternoon was a blur of phone calls and text messages, not unlike when someone has died, I guessed. ME's sister-in-law Caryl and I were back and forth a lot, and I left it to her to notify "the kids." They soon began calling or texting. All were caring and loving — for both ME and me. My call to ME's friend Joan was especially difficult. They had been friends more than 50 years; for the longest time, they talked almost every day. As ME's disease progressed, and she was less and less able to converse, Joan continued to call frequently. We had last seen her when we met in late May for ME's birthday lunch. Joan had given her a blue top from Talbots, which ME carried around for a while before I finally hung it, the tag still on. There were some tears during that call. And although I knew Joan understood the need for ME's move, I sensed that she struggled with its reality. I did not; I knew without a doubt that ME would be better off getting the care she needed from people who knew how to give it.

Late in the afternoon J emailed from WV to say ME was calm and cooperative. She attached three photos, each showing me that was so; my favorite was of ME on a bench outdoors talking with another resident. I shared the news with family members, something I would continue to do regularly in the days and weeks to come.

I had planned ahead for the evening and invited myself to dinner at Roberta and Sandra's. I don't recall what I said when I did that, but I know they had to be curious. They quickly knew something was wrong when I broke down shortly after we hugged a greeting. I could not catch my breath; words came haltingly as I cried, "I moved ME to memory care this morning." I apologized for not telling them — our dearest friends — in advance. "I couldn't risk something slipping out and alerting ME." More hugs. More tears. Best of all, they gave me the evening I needed, fed me and my soul. I allowed my emotions to just be. They listened patiently as I once more told the story in detail. They knew our journey well, and the support they offered me that night was more important than I can describe.

There were many others to notify, and I did that with emails over the next couple days. Rereading them, I can reconstruct more of what I was experiencing and feeling. To a neighbor, I included this: "WV is a wonderful place and my hope is that as the professionals get her acclimated, she will find some joy and peace in her days." To this day, that is what I ask for her each morning, along with her safety and health. I told my Uncle Delbert that I was "catching my breath, realizing how much time [caregiving] took, enjoying freedom from the [horrors] of the disease over these last months. I had less than a year of retirement before all this began, so now I have much to figure out."

To Jane, I wrote:

> As hard as I try, I cannot sit still or slow down. Already I realize how many things got pushed to the side in the last couple months as the demands of care grew and grew. . . . Right now it feels best to stay away to let her get acclimated. And I plan to check with them before I do go, because the last thing I want to cause is a setback in them gaining her trust. . . . As for me, I am trying to take it an hour at a time. I know I cannot rush adjusting to the "new normal," whatever that is. Everywhere I turn inside and outside the house there is neglect to undo. I have learned most things can wait awhile, so I can attend to self-care. I can read for pleasure, not escape. I do not have to fit the Y or shopping or appointments around the hours I have help. Whew. Eventually I should figure out how I want to be retired.

Were it not for the copious notes I wrote, I couldn't describe my first week alone. Wouldn't remember claiming the middle of the bed after too long sleeping on the edge, a pillow often wrapped around my head to muffle noise. Wouldn't remember snuggling with my stuffed bear, Packy, who has slept with me since. Wouldn't remember playing golf. Wouldn't remember feeling unfocused, adrift, fidgety. Wouldn't remember my first "unscripted day" when, fueled by adrenaline, I attacked tasks neglected too long. Wouldn't remember meeting with our financial advisor to tend to things for ME. Wouldn't remember that on just the fourth night — Thursday — I got a call from a WV nurse to tell me that ME apparently had fallen off the end of the bed. They had checked her out and she seemed OK, but they were doing their due diligence in informing me and asking if I wanted her taken to the hospital. I did not. I have to trust in the place, I concluded.

Were it not for the notes I wrote, I wouldn't know the details of the afternoon I visited ME for the first time. It was July 1, her first Saturday at WV. My heart, as it turned out, couldn't stay away too long. "Rattling around in the house surely is weird," I wrote to Sandra. "It will take time and lots of work, but I will make it mine." I was a bundle of nervous energy that morning. By 9 I had cleaned the den and downstairs bathroom, swept the kitchen, cleaned our tub and more. I had been to two markets. I gathered more pictures for ME's apartment and more clothes. I had texted J that I was nervous about visiting and asked if she had any advice. "Don't be nervous. . . ," she replied. "ME is in a better place emotionally and she will be happy to see you. Her comfort zone is actually expanding. . . ." Darlene concurred: "When I have stopped into WV, I see ME walking around without the 'babies.' Which is a clear sign she feels safe." To me, she said, "You need to give YOURSELF MUCH credit for taking this bold step for ME's wellbeing and quality of life for both of you." I kept that in mind as I left the house after lunch.

I timed the drive: 10 minutes. When I stopped first to see J, I learned ME had another fall. They suspected hydration might be an issue, perhaps compounded by her not eating much. That is what I had thought after she took two "tumbles" in the weeks before the move. J walked me to the dining area, and when I saw ME she looked so frail. She was hunched over in a chair, but when she spotted me and I greeted her with a hug, she cried. I held back my own tears as best I could. We walked to her room so I could show her what I had brought. The collage of old family photos brought more tears. I wondered if I should take it home, but J said no. "It will be OK."

J left us to visit. ME sat on her bed, fiddling with the blanket. (Perhaps it was a poor choice because it was soft and the fabric looked different depending how it was smoothed. I never thought of that; I chose it because it was purple, ME's favorite color.) I got her to walk to the courtyard, where we sat for a while. I brought her half a glass of lemonade, and when she drank it right down I got her another. I noticed that it took her awhile to get out of the chair; later I wondered if she had forgotten how. Back in her apartment, I got her settled in her recliner and gave her a Hershey's Kiss, happy that I had made that impulse purchase. J had asked to be with us when I was ready to leave. "I would like to be able to help you if she wants to go with you." She did not. Ever. That certainly made things easier for me.

At this early stage of our transitions, I went to sleep each night more confident about my decision to move ME and my choice of facility. I also realized that I had not fully grasped the nature of her placement in WV. Like residents in the larger assisted-living wing (which was part of an even larger complex of senior apartments), she was in an "apartment," albeit one large room with adjoining bathroom. The wing was locked, however, and the assistance and services she received were designed for individuals with memory issues. She was expected to walk to the dining room and was "free" to make as many decisions about herself as she was able.

Initially, J texted me regular updates about how ME was adjusting. I especially appreciated the candid photos she sent. In one from arrival day, she sat on a bench outdoors flanked by her purse and her "babies." She gazed directly into the camera, looking bemused. Another photo surprised me and everyone I showed it to: ME shooting a small basketball at a hoop.

What impressed me was how J and her staff worked to find ways to help ME adjust. Even when things were difficult, J was positive and reassuring. "I believe every day/evening from now on will be a bit easier until ME becomes familiar with us and the environment." Exactly! A day later, "She had a socially busy day, did bowling, had three good meals, and is getting more comfortable with other residents and staff. She also enjoys giving and receiving hugs." Reading that last sentence hurt. As much as it pains me to acknowledge, I had not offered many hugs in her last months at home.

The toughest nut to crack was her comfort level with personal care. No surprise there. J kept me informed, and I read her emails as just that, information. Those difficulties and all the others of the last many months no longer were mine to deal with or resolve. So when J told me about taking ME along with other residents to a local park, which did not go well, I just thanked her for trying. She suggested that WV was the environment where ME was comfortable and they would wait awhile before trying again. I said I hoped that would happen.

As for me, I wrote this about "the one-week mark of my new life, ME's new life, our new life. Yes, the choice I made, when finally necessity demanded it, is best for me, for her, for us. But that doesn't mean it always feels that way. Although in truth it mostly does. In the stillness of the early morning, as dawn approaches with its prelude to another day, I remember what was, mourn for what is, and am angry that what might have been, what could have been, will forever be a dream. Prevented by a cruel disease with only one outcome. The key to moving forward is acknowledging what is, living *in* the moment and *for* the moment. And that is what I am trying to do." Later that day, I was reminded how I was not always in charge of my own forward progress.

Early on the morning of July 4, I wrote of my gratitude "that ME is living in a place suited for her needs at this point in her life, but no longer independent. Grateful I am independent and taking baby steps toward a future not yet defined. But not at all independent of the great responsibility I have legally and feel emotionally — to ensure her safety and care." That pensiveness was connected to a call about 8 the night before. ME had fallen in the courtyard; they found her in the mulch. In my head, I saw her "frightened and confused on the ground. I also see her on Day 1, walking into WV unassisted, and the next day bowling. . . . What is going on?" The nurse who called said she had checked ME over and she seemed OK, except for some scrapes. We agreed that I would follow up with her primary care doctor after the holiday weekend. "This is all foreign to me, and I do not feel up to the task," I wrote. "But I must be."

As it turned out, my not feeling up to the task was just beginning. About 9 a.m. on the Fourth, I got a call from the WV nurse saying they were sending ME to the emergency room. They had trouble rousing her and it had taken three aides to get her up and dressed. So began my introduction to emergency medicine and hospitals — and on a holiday, to boot. (My only hospital stay was for a tonsillectomy, at age 5.) The first possibility offered was a stroke, so she had a CT scan, then a second one with contrast. No blockages, no bleeding, although I was told those facts could not definitively rule out stroke. They did bloodwork. No infection. The hospital's neurologist was not available, so the decision was made to admit her.

ME was remarkably calm through most of this, but she grimaced whenever her head was moved and she appeared to be in considerable pain. I acknowledged my own nervousness to every staff member I dealt with. Everyone in the ER was fantastic, and respectful of our relationship when I explained that I was ME's partner. They also were respectful of ME, careful not to speak only to me. At one point, as I was on the verge of losing it, a nurse hugged me and consoled me with as much tenderness as a friend would have. Later, I was quick to tell people that the doctor — a "hospitalist" — was the least impressive person we dealt with. When he first approached ME, he spoke much too loudly. She called him on it before I could. I loved that moment.

It took until 2:30 p.m. or so to get her a room. I learned that the plan was for a neurological consultation via teleconference, and so I hung around. It did not happen until about 5:15. Afterward, I was not sure how useful it had been, but ME seemed to do well with a couple of the tests. I answered a whole lot of questions as the doctor went through his checklist of why people fall. Bottom line: more tests needed.

I left after that, telling the nurse I would not likely be back for the evening. I was exhausted. I had not eaten a thing since 6:30 a.m. As I wrote to Sandra: "I am so out of my element on this one." I noted that an aide would help ME with her dinner, and that "I had to trust her care to the hospital. But I will soldier on and return in the morning to do my best to see that ME gets what she needs."

The next day was indeed a day of tests: heart ultrasound, MRI of head and neck, swallowing evaluation. I arrived about 8:30 a.m. to find ME had been moved to a room across from the nurses' station. I thought that was a good thing, because she needed that visibility. She was dozing and I saw that she had pulled out her IV, so I found a nurse to fix it. Her nurse, Shawna, impressed me more each time she was in the room. Over the course of the day, whenever I had stepped out so she could tend to ME, she always came to find me, to say, "She's all set, Barb." That small act went a long way toward helping me feel comfortable in an alien environment.

I remained at the ready, to be ME's voice and to ask my questions. I experienced the waiting and sitting and boredom I had only read about or seen on TV. I read, and when ME would wake I comforted her as best I could. When she was medicated in advance of the MRIs, I was able to get away for a couple hours. It allowed me to fetch a few badly needed groceries, then eat a quick lunch at home. I went to WV to pick up something for ME. J was not around, but I later updated her via email.

When I arrived back at the hospital, ME was still having lunch, and I was encouraged to see her eating a bit. For the rest of the afternoon, she slept and I hung out, afraid to miss something/someone important. Shawna delivered the good news that the MRIs showed no stroke. I expected that, but was relieved to have the confirmation. I ended up staying until almost 6, in hopes of seeing the spine doc, but that did not happen. I did meet with a discharge manager, who said ME likely would be released the next day. She had been in touch with the nurse at WV, and ME would be returned there as long as she were deemed safe.

ME was awake enough for dinner when it came about 5. I surprised myself by being able to feed her, and the busy aide thanked me for helping out. I appreciated that. Before I went home, I stopped at McDonald's for a takeout salad; I had no energy for cooking. I was emotionally drained. Sitting all day was anything but relaxing, but mostly it was the toll of caregiving. Once again I was where I did not expect to be, and although I believed that I had stepped up to the plate, it drained me. And then there was the profound sadness that swept over me. Sadness at seeing ME scared, helpless, drugged. My presence clearly had a positive, calming effect on her (most of the time), but I knew that I no longer could be that all the time, or even most of the time. I realized that I was afraid that the medical decision might be that she could not stay at WV, and if so, then what?!

After another restless night, I returned to the hospital about 8:30 Thursday. I was happy to see ME somewhat sitting up in bed. She had a good night, I was told, and there was noticeable improvement in her neck and her movement. When her pureed breakfast arrived, nurse Shawna quickly determined it wasn't needed (not to mention wasn't appealing). She fetched two pieces of French toast, which was a hit with ME. Later, she was dozing when a young woman from Physical Therapy stopped in. They really needed her up and walking. That took some doing, with me offering encouragement from the couch, but she and an aide got her — with a walker — to the door and back. ME made it clear that was all they were going to get!

The morning dragged on. ME looked at some TV, dozed, resumed looking at the TV, dozed. I waited for doctors who never came. An ultrasound of her carotid arteries had been ordered and finally I was told it would not happen until afternoon. Another tech came in to do a blood pressure test of her lying down, sitting up and standing. All was good. She cooperated and was able to swing her legs off the bed and get herself standing with only a bit of help. I was encouraged. I also was encouraged when she ate some of her lunch without help. I think she liked the attention of being fed, however, so I helped her as she ate her entire serving of chocolate pudding (Ms. Sweet Tooth, still). Then she dozed again. I hoped to get away for a couple hours, but waited lest I miss the case manager. Thank goodness for the latest John Grisham on my Kindle.

Finally, again having seen no one, I went home, put my feet up and closed my eyes for a few minutes reprieve from "hospitaling." When I returned, I almost ran into the case manager as I rounded a hallway. She updated me on the timing of ME's discharge and said she was ordering her a walker. When I got to her room, they were just getting ready to take her for the test I expected she would be returning from. I stayed with her until she was wheeled away, then headed to WV. I hoped to talk with the nursing director about her care needs, and I got lucky; she was available. I authorized "whatever it takes" to return her to "baseline" relatively quickly. I also wanted to know if she thought I should be there when ME arrived. I admit to being relieved when she said, "Let us bring her back to us." With that, I left for home.

I sent a text to update the family. A couple hours later, I sent another: "More encouraging news. The nursing director (H) called about 5:15 to say ME had arrived. She got off the stretcher on her own. Was glad to see her babies in her room. H asked if she wanted to take a walk to the dining room with her, which she did. Sat right down and began eating dinner. H thought she was more mobile than she had expected. I am breathing a bit easier." Then I got an email from J who, although off work, went in to help out for the evening: "ME . . . looks very happy to be back. She hugged and kissed me when she saw me. Right now she is watching TV and is very content." I felt a weight lift from my shoulders. I was off the roller coaster. Until the next time.

I slept better that night, knowing ME was safely "home." But better is a relative term; 6 a.m. was preferable to 4:30 or 5, but not enough to prevent me from later falling asleep in my recliner. I tried to be grateful for whatever sleep I did get, and was grateful for no bad-news phone call. Out of necessity, by this time I had a new relationship with telephones. In the past, I was content to monitor calls via the answering machine and pick up only if I wanted to. I often did not carry my cell phone. Now I answered the house phone promptly and *always* carried my cell.

ME's crisis took me almost back to square one in adjusting to being alone. Oddly, one thing those three days gave my days was meaning and purpose. I would re-find that, I knew. On this day I was content to meet Sandra for coffee; the good fellowship and her steady support over the months were a real gift. Then I tried to take the day slowly. I was beyond tired, so when a task occurred to me, I asked myself whether it had to be done immediately, and generally answered no. I did go to the Y, which I had missed. But when I contemplated buying fish to cook for dinner, I decided I did not have the energy for that. I allowed myself a lazy day in all ways, including the first day since starting Weight Watchers (on May 4) that I did not eat well or mindfully. The world did not end.

I remained bone weary on Saturday, but I was determined to go to

Connecticut for a family picnic. It would be my first time seeing folks without ME; our last trip there had been Easter. Emotionally fragile, I was buoyed by hugs and conversations, saddened by a couple people who seemed unable to ask me about ME. I had gone intending to stay until mid-afternoon, which is what I did. We were squeezed indoors because of the heat and humidity, and finally it was too chaotic for me. On the drive back to Rhode Island, I took the "scenic" route paralleling the interstate. ME and I almost always chose this, and so there were memories all along the way. I allowed them to wash over me as I listened to the Red Sox game. It had been important to me to "represent" ME at the gathering. What I realized on the drive home was that it also had been important to go for me.

The next day, I shared news of the picnic when I visited ME. I had been both eager and apprehensive about visiting; my stomach still tightened up each time I walked from my car to the front door. Finding her took some doing; she liked visiting other residents' rooms, I was told. She looked good, but she was not using her walker. The staff said she resisted it, and they could not force her. I, on the other hand, had no qualms about insisting she use it as we walked the hallways. I begged her to use it so she would not fall again (almost everyone else there used some sort of walking aid, after all). Oops, still trying to reason with her. Old habits die hard. Ditto for reminding her that her nephew and family, who live in Kansas, would be visiting the next day.

They first came to the house, and we had lunch out before going to WV. They knew about ME's hospitalization, but our time allowed me to give them an idea of what to expect. I so wanted it to go well for everyone. They were her first visitors, and I could see in her eyes that she was happy.

I was not happy that she was in a nightgown, but proud of myself for not making an issue about it.

It took a bit of doing, but I got her to take my arm and we all went to the dining room, where we commandeered a table big enough for all eight of us. ME loved playing peek-a-boo with her youngest grand-nephew, and the other two found puzzles they put together for her. She got a silly smirk on her face when she upended one and the pieces fell out. We took photos before heading back to her apartment. The boys loved her babies, but when one asked if he could change an outfit, ME said "better not." Our leave-taking was done without fuss, ME content in her chair, holding a baby. I arrived home heartened by the love and respect she received that afternoon.

Now it was time to re-focus on me. I was impatient to get on with it, whatever it might be. I prepared for a trip to Wisconsin and time with my family. I bought a new front door, so I would not have to switch out storm and screen, a task I could not handle alone. I scheduled the installation of ductless air-conditioning. I promised myself a new TV. I prepared to sell ME's car. I marveled at being able to make a decision without "a lot of hoo-ha." In therapy sessions, I found myself communicating with a clarity that amazed me. I tried to take to heart Beverly's advice to be patient, that adjusting to my "now" life would take time. I needed to trust myself and my feelings. I put it this way: "It is important that I allow myself to feel *whatever* it is I am feeling, knowing there will be all sorts of emotions in the days, weeks, months ahead."

I had buried my feelings for so long, subsumed my emotional needs to ME's. How long had it been, for example, that I had only myself to think about when traveling? (When I made plans to spend a week in Wisconsin,

I did not know ME would be in memory care.) Of course I would think about her while away, and I would be concerned that her days went well. "But I don't have to WORRY; the professionals are taking good care of her," I wrote. It was important for me to remember that the goal for people with dementia is not their happiness, the goal is that they be safe and well cared for. It is a sentiment I shared often. Understanding its truth was a gift. "So," my note ended, "here's to a terrific vacation. I am not taking my iPad; if I write notes at all, they will be brief and, I trust, without drama. As I hope my life can be for a while."

It was.

Back home and in a particularly reflective mood on the last Saturday of July, I addressed my morning note directly to ME. I find it among the most powerful summations of my feelings and am glad to have it.

It is 5:42 a.m. I have been up since 5:10, awake since 4. Not so long ago, this early morning quiet was my refuge. Now it is just quiet. Then I drank my coffee, read, and hoped you would not awake and come downstairs until at least 8. I resented it when you were early. Now it is just quiet.

I have begun to realize how unprepared I was/am for the changes forced on us by your disease. In your last weeks at home, I was so worn down by your agitation and anger that I could barely function. I closed myself off from you even more than I had, my coping mechanism against the hurt I felt. You were lost to me, lost to yourself, and the rare moments that felt like the 'old days' could not counterbalance the present. But . . . you were the other beating heart in the house. And that was something. Now only one heart beats here. And five weeks into our "new normal" (I first wrote "the," but that was not personal and this is) I have regained enough perspective to feel the hurt from that fact.

I wanted space and now I have it, but I have yet to figure out what to do with it. Sometimes I wonder, if we had had a larger circle of friends, would this be easier. I think not; this is my journey. A journey I never imagined. Twenty-seven years of partnership, of sharing, of life lived together. Even the almost four years from diagnosis to now were done together — though not as well as they could have been, I see now. Our personal "weaknesses" were magnified: your refusing to acknowledge your disease, your "dark" view of the world and people, your indecision, your need to be perfect, your extreme privacy. My need to take charge, to try to fix things, to reason and not feel, to shut down, to do things my way, to back away from unpleasant tasks until there was no option but to do them.

Now you are minutes away, physically, but miles in reality. I no longer need to be the fixer, the problem solver — and yet I do. I am, for better or worse, a partner in your care. And it seems to require some part of my day each day, so it remains difficult to carve out time for my recharging, my healing. There are the tasks that legal guardianship require. There are the things like selling your car, dealing with insurance, dealing with doctors. Not to mention visiting and finding you in need of [something that] demonstrates your reluctance for personal care. My assistance is requested, and while it is of some help, I leave concerned that your (disease's) behavior will force you out of WV. I fight to live in the moment, which is them still committed to figuring out what will work. I fight to tamp down my own fear of being forced into another monumental choice for you. I fight to take it one day at a time.

I need not wonder why I still wake so early.

August marked the start of month two of my "new" life. I reflected on that in a long email to Jane, beginning, "I realized not too long ago how unprepared I was" for my change in status. "I was so burned out . . . that all I wanted was to be done with [caregiving]." Once that happened, "there was great relief — and sadness. But then her hospitalization after just a week rebooted the turmoil." It was a setback for ME's adjustment to WV; personal care continued to be a battle. I was worried, I told Jane, because "it is imperative she allow them to help her, because it is assisted living and not a nursing home."

Her decline was visible, I told Jane. When I saw a year-old Facebook photo and then one of ME and Mike at WV, I was taken aback. But my fear of not being recognized had not materialized; indeed, there were times when she greeted me, "Hi honey." We enjoyed walking in the courtyard, and although it reminded me of her fall, that was my issue alone. Her "babies" still brought her obvious comfort. I understand that family members sometimes balk at giving a doll to their adult loved one, but I never did. I became quite good at role-playing when ME tended to them.

"Meanwhile," I told Jane, "as I work on my own recovery and replenishing, every day there seems to be an ME-related task." My least favorite — and most time consuming — was preparing the required detailed inventory of her assets. At least I learned about appraisers, Fair Market Value and the like. What a disappointment to pay $500 to learn that the two antique rugs ME thought were valuable actually *might* fetch $675!Finally, I continued to see myself as one half of a couple, evident in the closing of my email to Jane: "Love to you both, from both of us."

ME's continued resistance to help with personal care remained perplexing. J and the staff were determined to find the key to unlocking that door. I could not help but feel anxious about it. Sweet, gentle ME, who could surprise J by "sneaking" up to her from behind and hugging her, could also stubbornly push back at anyone trying to help her. Once, when the administrator asked me how things were, and I remarked on that, she said simply: "That's why we're here." My response: "That's what I try to remember."

With my therapist's help, I learned to "debrief" myself when there were unsettling parts of a visit with ME. Before driving away, I would acknowledge aloud what had upset me, how I responded, and give myself credit for a reasonable response. I worked to let toxic feelings go in hopes of keeping myself from rehashing things over and over. What I wanted to carry with me — to *not* forget — were the "settled" moments. Bringing ice cream. Sewing a button on a sweater (thank goodness for 4-H). Reframing a favorite photo of her with her oldest brother. Paging through her alumni magazine together. Walking in the courtyard and admiring the flowers and shrubs and butterflies while avoiding the bees. Hearing her say something to another resident. Watching her respond to staff who, to a person and regardless of job, called her by name.

Nonetheless, it felt to me like moving ME out of the house had not freed me from demands for my time, at least not to the extent I expected. I imagined, naively I suppose, that once she was in memory care I would not experience such angst. But I continued to feel the sharp tug of responsibility, felt that I must continue to put ME's needs first. I recall talking at length about that in therapy, looking for a way to handle my churning stomach and anxiety.

In late August, after a particularly difficult afternoon, I was relieved by an email from J reporting that ME had eaten a good dinner, had a good evening followed by a good morning, and was taking a walk. That all changed with a 4 a.m. phone call on Saturday, August 26. They had found ME on the floor, scalp bloody, and sent her to the ER to be checked out. Groggy me said I was not going to the hospital and would check in with WV later. Within a few minutes I knew that was unacceptable, so I quickly dressed and drove the 15 minutes to the hospital. ME seemed calm, but a thin-skin bruise on her arm was bleeding and she had a cut on the top of her head. A CT scan showed all was OK. The doctor thought two staples to close the scalp cut would be easier on her than stitches, and I said do it. I never will forget how she cried out with each staple; thankfully the procedure was quick. She was transported back to WV before 7 and I returned home.

I was a wreck. What a roller coaster! I repeatedly told myself, "It's not about you." I went home with ME's shirt. It took some doing, but I got the blood out, and about 10:30 decided to drive over to see how she was doing. I also hoped that we might figure out where she fell and what she could have hit her head on. I found her asleep in a dining room chair. I worked my magic and helped the staff rouse her and get her to her room. Afterward, I walked her to the TV room and sat with her a bit. I left before lunch with assurances that she would eat. I was certain she was exhausted. I know I was physically and emotionally spent.

Sunday was fall-like, the morning cloudless. I wrote about how I did not want summer to end, "though I am calling this The Lost Summer." I had slept unusually well; exhaustion can do that to a person. "The question of this morning is, How to make peace with what is? . . . Maybe roller coaster is the new normal, and I don't have to enjoy the ride as much as accept that as I continue on it." After all, I was just two months removed from direct caregiving.

Ninety minutes of yard work — accomplishing something visible — energized me. I washed up, determined to do serious work in my gardens before late fall. My important lesson was that I could do it a little bit at a time, on *my* schedule. So I decided to visit ME after lunch.

I brought her a dried hydrangea bloom from our yard in a San Xavier candle jar that I fashioned into a vase. I thought she would enjoy both the flower and its container, from one of our Tucson vacations. ME was dozing, but I nudged her awake. A young man was playing guitar and singing in the living room, and I persuaded her to go with me. We stayed for the hour, and when ME began singing along or clapping to the rhythm, it brought me close to tears. This was what I had hoped for her at WV. Why hadn't I done this with her before? Why was it so difficult for me?

After the music, we walked a few loops around the courtyard, then joined other residents for "happy hour." We are actually having fun, I thought. We went back outside for a couple more loops before I settled her into a living room chair with a magazine. I had stayed about two hours. It was good. It felt right. It was a breakthrough for me, that I could choose to join her *when I wanted* and she might adjust even better. I vowed that I would pay attention to the special-events calendar and make a point of trying to share activities with her.

I never got that chance.

Monday's weather again was glorious, and I resumed my outdoor work by clearing a spot so I could finally plant the Scotch Broom that I had bought so many weeks before. ME had been with me on that shopping trip. I also had a long chat with a neighbor whose father-in-law had dementia. I learned that he had recently been moved to yet another nursing home as they struggled to find him the right placement. Once again I thought about how lucky I was to have ME at WV.

Finally back in the house mid-afternoon, I had an email from J. It was not good news. The roller coaster I thought was finally on a straightaway was beginning another descent. J explained that ME was being evaluated by the nurse because she had complained of leg pain. She said the nurse would call with an update. It turned out that on Sunday night, the staff had found ME sitting by her bed and holding her right leg. Monday morning they found her again sitting on the bed and not ready to get up. She said her leg hurt. They got her to lie down and she slept on and off until almost noon. When it was time for lunch, she could not put weight on her leg to stand. When the nurse finally called, it was to say they were sending ME to the hospital.

The roller coaster was picking up speed. I got to the emergency room about 4:30; ME arrived a bit after 5. The place was a zoo. ME was alert, generally calm, and clearly in discomfort. There proved to be *lots* of waiting over the course of the evening and into the night. An X-ray of her right hip was negative. Wait. A CT scan was ordered, but first she had to be sent back to her ER space and put on special blow-up mattress that makes transfer easier and more comfortable. Wait. Out again for the scan. Wait.

After several minutes, a technician came to ask for my help; ME's pain as they tried to position her caused agitation. I was able to get her to hold my hands and thus get her arms out of the way. They got me a big lead apron to wear during the scan (now that is something I never expected to do!). More waiting. Scan showed no fracture. Eventually the hospitalist (a young woman) stopped by to say she was going to consult an orthopedist about ordering an MRI. So ME was admitted — but no bed was available.

I learned that the emergency room was at the time a "holding pen" for eight or nine patients. ME was lucky to be in a cubicle by herself. The plan was to bring her a regular bed for the night, so I needed to wait for that to happen. I was hesitant to leave other than to pee (Ha. I knew where the bathroom was because of Saturday's ER trip.) because ME couldn't communicate to anyone stopping in. I was so hungry, and so wishing I had brought a Clif bar (at least I had my Kindle). Someone eventually pointed me to a vending machine; a package of peanut butter crackers offered a bit of protein. (I actually scanned it for Weight Watchers points.) It was late night before the bed arrived, and once ME was resettled I left. I arrived home about 12:45 a.m. Tuesday.

As exhausted as I was, I awoke about 4 and finally got up about 5. I had texted Libby late Monday that I was unlikely to make golf or the year-end luncheon. Sigh. I confirmed that with another text about 6. I also had kept WV updated, but had not yet contacted family. I wanted to have something definitive to share. I think I read a bit; I know I drank two cups of coffee instead of my usual one (as the day progressed, I was very happy to know where the bathroom was).

When I returned to the ER about 8:30, ME was dozing. I was told she had an OK night. They brought her breakfast and she ate a few bites of egg and half an English muffin (at least she more or less fed herself, which during her July stay she had not done) until she just could not stay awake. The hospitalist came by to confirm the MRI — time unknown. Had I seen the orthopedist, she asked. No. She must have checked on ME very early. By then, I also had learned that the hospital was in "diversion mode"; no more ambulances were being accepted until all the ER patients waiting on beds got one. The morning dragged on.

One bright spot had its origin in a spur-of-the-moment email I had sent on Sunday. Something I read had prompted me to contact the church ME had attended to ask if the pastor might visit her at WV. Why I had not thought of that before was a mystery. I suggested that although she had not joined the parish, she had attended Mass almost weekly, and the pastor might remember her because of their Irish connection. In addition, ME had known the substitute priest for decades. "ME's faith was always important to her (she had four uncles who were priests)," I wrote, "and I believe she would find comfort in visits." Now the pastor had written to say he remembered ME "very well" and was sorry to hear about her condition. He said he would see her at WV on Wednesday morning. I immediately wrote back to tell him of her hospitalization, said I hoped "she will not have to stay long," and promised to be in touch about his visit.

Finally, the MRI happened and revealed a "hidden" fracture in ME's right hip, so surgery would be scheduled. I was surprised to learn that the MRI also showed a cyst on one kidney. Yikes! One problem at a time, I thought, before leaving for eggs at my favorite diner and a quick stop at home. When I returned to the hospital, ME still was waiting for a room. I got her lunch reheated and was happy when she ate much of it before nodding off.

As ME slept, a case manager stopped by. Like almost everyone I had been dealing with, she was pleasant. She told me she would get people working on finding a post-surgery rehab spot for ME. (Yet another set of changes to come. Arghhh.) ME continued to sleep soundly. I sat and sat and sat. I read. When an aide came to tend to her, I ventured outside to move my car to a closer parking spot. It felt good to get fresh air.

Late in the afternoon, ME was again asleep and I had closed my eyes. There was a tap on the cubicle door. It was the pastor! I gently tried to wake ME, but nothing doing. He asked if it was OK to say the prayer for the sick. Of course, I said. I may not be a believer, but his act of kindness had me choked up because I knew how appreciative ME would be.

A couple more hours passed before a nurse came in to say there finally was a bed for ME, and shortly after she was transported to 305. It had been 24 hours since she arrived at the ER. I hung around another hour or so, until the nurse had gotten the intake information she needed. She was able to tell me that the surgery was scheduled for the next day, likely late because ME was an add-on to the schedule. On my way home, I grabbed a WW-friendly Subway sandwich. I got a call from an anesthesiologist and gave the necessary consent. I turned on the Red Sox game to watch as I updated people via texts. Somehow I remembered to cancel a repair appointment I had scheduled for early Wednesday. Finally, I tried to unwind before bed, hoping for more sleep than the night before.

I did make it to 6 a.m., but the last hour or so was restless. I found it difficult to keep my mind from negative spaces. I had read enough to know about the pitfalls of surgery for dementia patients and the challenges rehab would present. Back at the hospital about 8:45, I found one of my golf pals volunteering at the front desk, and we chatted. ME was semi-awake when I arrived. I immediately noticed the IV was in her other arm, and deduced that she had a rough night. A "therapy apron" rested on her lap, probably an attempt to distract her. I asked to speak with her nurse, but that wouldn't happen for a while. So we watched some news.

An aide came to take her for a kidney ultrasound. I waited in the atrium and read *The New York Times*. Back in her room, ME dozed. A pharmacist stopped in to check on meds, which I reviewed with her (like most of the staff, she looked so young, although many of the nurses this time around were more "mature"). At last I met with her nurse; she said they were not able to do the ultrasound. Later, when the hospitalist came by, I asked about that. It can wait, she said, assuring me its purpose was simply to better define the cyst. I got a text from Libby wondering if I wanted a coffee break. I begged off, saying I needed to do some errands. I got away before noon, promising to return by 2, when ME would go to pre-op.

My first stop was home, to find a glasses case for ME and write a check to hold her WV apartment for September. I opted for lunch out because I wanted a real meal and figured that by day's end I would be too tired for one. The restaurant was near WV, so after I ate I dropped off the check and updated J. She gave me a big hug, as did an aide.

Back at the hospital. ME was restless and hungry. Taking her to pre-op about 2 proved to be much too early. A nurse summoned me from the waiting room to answer questions and sit with ME for a while. I worked my magic and calmed her. Eventually they sent me back to the waiting room (thankfully fairly empty and quiet) until once again I was called in, this time to meet with the anesthesiologist. He did an excellent job explaining things and I agreed to general anesthesia. I stayed and held ME's hand while they gave her the first med. Her nurse was an older man, who was gentle with her and patiently explained every move to me. Finally I was off to wait. And wait. And wait. I read, but was more and more distracted as time wore on. The television's Judge Judy was annoying. So was the local news that followed. So was the family of four that arrived, sat in four corners and talked — loudly.

I became anxious when it seemed as if the surgery should have been finished. The second half hour of the news began, and I worried. At last the surgeon came out and flashed me a thumbs-up from across the room. Everything went as planned, he said, explaining that ME would be in Recovery awhile, then taken to her room. He expected that she would sleep until morning. Relieved and thankful I headed to my car, where I composed and sent this text: "She's in Recovery. All went well. Small incision. Can put weight on it right away. Likely to mostly sleep into tomorrow. I am going home."

I added that last sentence because I did not want to have to answer phone calls. I got thankful texts in return, but no calls. Libby wondered about getting dinner; needing alone time, I declined. I assembled a simple meal for myself, turned on the Red Sox game, and sat in my recliner under a quilt (I shiver when nervous — or exhausted). Before long, I fell soundly asleep. I emerged from that "nap" slowly and remained in my chair until after 9, when I dragged myself upstairs for a bit more TV until sleep returned.

The next morning (Thursday), having smartened up and brought my iPad to the hospital, I sent a text with these details: "Arrived hospital about 8:30. ME was having breakfast. She looks good, is alert. Her nurse said she had a good night. All post-op vitals are good. I took over feeding her. (I think she enjoys the attention, but I hope she will feed self at lunch.) There was enough food on the tray for a lumberjack, and she ate well (her last meal had been Tuesday about 2). Now dozing. Will update you when I know more."

I was relieved by how I found her. Cognitively, I judged, she was close to baseline. She clearly recognized me, greeted me with "Hi Honey," and I saw little to no evidence of delirium. She smiled at kids on TV and dozed comfortably. They were not giving her narcotics, which I had hoped could be the case. "As for me," I wrote in a note, "I was awake at 4 but got myself back to sleep until about 6. Apprehension as I emerged from sleeping and got myself going. Did not read, decided I needed to write. Proud of myself that before I left the house I got online to make the Hurricane Harvey donation I said I was going to do yesterday. Now it is hanging out and waiting to see what develops."

I finished writing my account of the day later:

> PT came in mid-morning to get ME up and into chair, with help of walker (and me). Took some doing, but she got to her feet (first time since Sunday evening, I believe) and surprised us all by walking. Steered her toward door, out a few steps into hall, and actually had to stop her! Got her settled in chair and we hung out watching TV. She commented appropriately a couple times, laughed at kids. Also dozed, which was good for her. Nurse Pam later unhooked her from IV and removed catheter.

During PT, a case manager came by and we stepped into hall,

which upset ME. It is a heavy burden to have her well-being so seemingly dependent on me, and it grows with each day in this circumstance. But because she cannot speak for herself, I feel I need to be a constant presence for her. I did leave for a while, to get lunch and go to WV to meet with their doctor to explore making him ME's doctor. I decided to do so. Surprisingly, at McDonald's a group from WV was eating lunch.

Back at the hospital, more sitting. I ran into case manager in the hall and discharge will be tomorrow to SKNRC, about 15 minutes from the house. . . . Hospitalist stopped in to check vitals etc. As afternoon wore on, I thought ME was more restless and fidgety. More verbal, too, but seldom made sense. Guessing some impact from the anesthesia. She also cried when case manager stopped in to answer my questions about tomorrow. Not sure she understood us, but something triggered tears. Afterward I wondered if she had some pain. I left about 4. I was emotionally spent; her crying really got to me. I hate that there needs to be yet another change of location for her, but it can't be helped. It is taking a toll on me, too. Stopped by WV to get her some clothes, picked up some dinner, got home, sent update text. Now it is time to stop writing and try to unwind, to think of anything but all of this.

Throughout ME's hospitalization and after, I couldn't help but think of our happy Sunday together, how she had walked with me in the courtyard. Had it been too much? I eventually concluded that the leg pain she had complained about for months was because of that tiny fracture, which probably was related to osteoporosis. The dots from the "tumbles" before memory care to her recent falls connected for me. I had not done anything wrong. Her caregivers had not, either. The damn disease was the culprit. I needed to direct my energy to ensuring that her rehabilitation prepared her to return to WV. After that, I could return to moving my own life forward.

". . . if we dealt honestly with our emotions and recognized them for what they were — symptoms of loss — it would enable us to pull wisdom and meaning from pain. [As Tomlinson said] 'It will deepen and strengthen our relationship with ourselves and increase our resilience in living. That is Janet's gift to us, but we must choose to accept her gift'."

Spoken at the memorial for Janet
in *Twelve-Mile Limit*
Randy Wayne White

CHAPTER 8

Rediscovering Love

At 6:10 a.m. on Friday, September 1, I summed up my reality this way:

A new day. A new month. I started to write "a new chapter in this journey," but decided that is not accurate. The chapter just continues, with one of those breaks between sections. I greeted the world an hour ago with a request for strength for today — physical, emotional, mental — and thanks for realizing how much I need those. Then I tried reading, wanting to not immediately immerse myself in my anxiety over what lies ahead. I forced myself to get out of bed when I found it was counterproductive to fight those anxieties. They had crept in when I awoke about 3, and they returned immediately when I awoke again about 5.

This transition feels different than the move to memory care. Then I just needed to be out of the caregiving role. Love was hiding; only a sense of responsibility kept me going. Now, just as love resurfaced, I feel battered about. I am exhausted by the responsibility of monumental decisions. I am scared that I have relied too much on the professionals, agreed too quickly to the rehab facility. I can only hope that seeing it today, getting ME "'settled" will bring a bit of relief. But I doubt it, since it is a holiday weekend and who knows what that means for staffing.

I need to dig deep and figure out how to advocate for her best interests. I still believe that is WV — asap. But is she up to the PT that will be required, and can this place get her there? I also have to dig deep and yet again begin to reclaim myself. Feels as if I am not back to square one, but the square before that. Ouch.

And to top things off, a pesky bed slat fell when I got out of bed and I had to figure out how to get it back in place — no easy task alone.

I found it ironic that the ruse we used when moving ME to memory care was that she was going to get rehab for her leg, and this day's move really was for rehab! But first, several more hours at the hospital. Going there felt only slightly more comfortable than my first trips, but at least I now knew my way around, recognized some staff, knew something about the routines. That sense of minimal comfort was about to change.

In the text I wrote to family at the end of the day, I started by saying, "ME is a trouper! It has been a long day, at the end of a long week with way more changes and confusion than she deserves. And she is hanging in there." Rereading that, I believe I should have added "and so am I."

Leaving the hospital was about as easy as could be, I guess. I had arrived about 8:45, and ME began her journey to SKNRC about 1:30, after lunch. The discharge planner had arranged the placement, and I agreed because it had a locked dementia unit and was close to home. The PT people said they send lots of folks there with good results, so that was reassuring. They told me three to six weeks was typical for rehabilitation after surgery such as hers. The goal was to get her "safely mobile." That was my goal for her too, so she could return to WV.

Getting checked in to SKNRC was time consuming, but everyone I dealt with was kind and helpful. Everyone was also extremely busy. It was Friday afternoon of Labor Day weekend, the dementia unit was near capacity and, if I recall, there were two other "admits" in addition to ME.

If not my worst nightmare, walking into the building was indeed a nightmare. If hospitals had been foreign territory for me when summer began, rehab facilities were uncharted (I did not call it a nursing home). I did not know until a transport person mentioned they had just taken ME's roommate there that she would have a roommate. My bad for not asking. The dementia wing is at the back, so I had to walk through what I called "the nursing home part." And, to be honest, I called it "awful" in my notes that night. The dementia wing is called PondView, and indeed it has a pond view. I also saw "a lot of people in more advanced stages of disease than ME." I gritted my teeth so as not to "show my horror to her." It was so much more chaotic than WV; I hoped ME would be able to sleep. Already I was thinking ahead: "Should she not be able to go back to WV, or when the time comes that she has to leave, I will do my damndest to find someplace different than this." I think I was in shock; the admissions director told me months later that I had the "deer in headlights" look. Undoubtedly I would have reacted negatively to *any* facility that day.

I stayed with ME until after supper. I wondered if she knew the fish sandwich was her second such meal that day. There had been a lot of paperwork for me, first with the admissions person, then with the social worker, then with the PondView nurse. I signed where I was instructed, assured the social worker I would not require help with Medicaid forms any time soon, and made choices about what level of care ME should get in case of illness. I swallowed hard before checking the DNR box.

I returned Saturday morning in order to be available when the PT director assessed ME. It was nice to see her dressed after days of hospital gowns. Once we got her to stand, she took off with the walker, surprising him (and me) with how far she went. He said stamina clearly was not an issue, so they would work on balance, strengthening her lower body and repaired hip. He said she would get therapy five days a week, and I told him to "push her because she is a trouper."

After a badly needed lunch with my friend Libby, I returned to ME mid-afternoon. She was in a wheelchair in the Activities Room, watching "Daddy Day Care" with several others. I trimmed and filed her nails — a first for me — which seemed to make her happy. I surprised myself when I realized how much I enjoyed being able to do that for her. When she started to doze, I said a quiet goodbye. On my way out, the nurse told me that "she is adjusting well" and had enjoyed two servings of ice cream at lunch. I was not surprised. If only I felt that I were adjusting.

But I *had* taken two important steps for myself that Saturday. I went to a morning Weight Watchers meeting and in the late afternoon I made it to the Y. Although I had not yet recognized Weight Watchers and the YMCA as gifts from ME's dementia, each had become vital to my moving forward. The Y had come first, and was a habit helping both my physical and mental health. Each time I finished a bike ride I said, "Good girl; I'm proud of you" aloud to myself. I had joined WW on May 4. I struggled with weight most of my life, and like so many people had lost and gained and lost and gained more times than I could count. Given my dislike of "groups," WW was not an obvious choice, but I think now that it was a sign of how desperate I felt. Not necessarily desperate to lose weight, but to do something — *anything* — to take some control of my life. I was inspired by Libby's success; she is a few years older than I, and I figured if she could do it so could I.

Sunday I wrote about feeling "basically back to the beginning" in needing to "replenish my battery," as my therapist described what I was going through. I thought my caregiver title could be retired after ME's move to memory care, but quickly learned it could not. "The difference now is that I understand . . . what *I* need and I am giving myself permission to do it," I wrote.

By Monday — Labor Day — "the depth of my fatigue" had lessened, "but just a bit. It is both physical and emotional." I blamed that fatigue for my failure to hit the "send" button on the message I wrote to update family on ME's status. And that was before the day's visit with her. She had not had a good morning; she fought care and did not eat breakfast. When I arrived she was in a wheelchair in the main room, no eyeglasses, and wearing a shirt that turned out to be her roommate's. The nightstand that was supposed to be in her room still had not arrived. Is there any wonder why my stomach was in knots? I needed to be patient, for sure, but I also needed to advocate on ME's behalf. There was no guidebook to instruct me; I had to figure out for myself how to be a secondary caregiver.

As I write now, it feels silly to include my out-of-proportion, stomach-churning upset over laundry, but to tell my story honestly I must. At check-in, I had opted for "family will do laundry" even before I knew the facility sent out its laundry — great quantities of laundry, what with linens, towels and clothing — and it takes a week for it to be returned. I was complaining about items missing from ME's closet and not in her laundry basket. I was told things might show up in the next delivery. I was skeptical and vowed not to bring any more clothes to her if I could help it — thinking of the probable length of her rehab stay.

Fortunately, I had a therapy session a few days after ME was admitted to SKNRC. I know I talked about laundry before anything else, including my angst, my lost summer (What kind of karma was at work that ME's medical emergencies happened over July Fourth and Labor Day?), my apprehension every time I drove to SKNRC. "Just roll with the waves," Beverly motioned when, at the end of the session I asked, "Any advice?" So that is what I tried to do, that and listen to my heart. When that advice had been offered as I left ME at WV, my heart needed to stay away, to have distance from caregiving. Now my heart needed to see that ME was all right, was getting what she needed in order to be discharged. Even if my discomfort led to short visits, I was able to hug her, kiss her, say I would be back. Those were not words or actions I had offered for the longest time.

About the same time, I had this "ah ha" moment: Could it be that ME does not feel the discomfort with SKNRC that I do? I had not seen her agitated, and I continued to describe her as a trouper. I said as much to her brother Mike and sister-in-law Caryl when they visited for the first time. Being with them for a couple hours did me as much good as it did ME. Perhaps it was not having to walk into the facility alone. Perhaps it was having them tell me I was doing well, and not feeling reproach for choosing the place. Perhaps it was our pleasant visit in the blessedly quiet back room.

Whatever, it left me feeling more mellow than I had in ages. That night, my Fitbit told me, I slept almost nine hours, with just 34 minutes awake/restless. Only a couple of nights before, it had been 90 minutes of awake/restless.

ME had a follow-up appointment with her surgeon on September 11. Getting her there proved challenging, despite my having made arrangements well in advance. And once again a lot of waiting was involved. We eventually made it to the office, except they did not seem to be expecting us. We waited. They sent her for an X-ray (didn't know that would happen), followed by a quick check from the doctor and the okay to continue physical therapy without restriction. The office called for a transport. More waiting. We finally made it back to SKNRC about 11:30. Whew! ME had said she was hungry, so I made that point to a staff member. But I could not stay to see if she got a snack because I was meeting a friend for lunch. I kept expecting things to work "the way they are supposed to," and planned my life accordingly. Would I ever learn? Apparently not.

Only a day later, I found myself saying again how "I hate roller coasters!" — my latest ride precipitated by "the system" not working. Maybe I should have been prepared for a battle with health-care bureaucrats, but that world was totally new to me. I was clueless. When the social worker called to tell me Medicare was cutting off ME's coverage after 10 days, I was incredulous. Medicare had determined that her dementia prevented her from cooperating for rehab; it would quit paying after September 14. How could this be? The surgeon said she was on track with PT, and I knew her own insurance policy covered a lot more days.

The news sent me into a tailspin; why did everything have to be so difficult, I wondered. I spent the evening fuming and worrying. What the hell was I going to do? Eventually I talked myself down from the ledge, figuring ME would not be tossed out. I assumed she would become "private pay" for the short term while I got things straightened out. Thank goodness the money for care is there, I thought, knowing how fortunate that made us. None of this helped me sleep better, however.

The social worker had given me the contact information I needed to dispute the decision. By the end of the next day, I counted myself among the thousands of people made to feel helpless by the system. "I have a Ph.D.," I thought again and again. "I should be able to figure this out." Ha. I made my first call to the company that manages Medicare appeals at 9:30 a.m. Suffice it to say the rest of the day was a series of long waits for calls to be returned, missed messages, lack of communication. When, late that afternoon, I finally reached a real person, I at last was able to tell ME's story — how she had been moved to rehab on a holiday weekend, what I had seen her do, how the dementia complicated working with her but did not prevent it, that the surgeon declared her on track. In short, I said, the rehab folks had not given her enough time and Medicare's assessment was premature. She took the information and informed me I would have an answer to my appeal in 24 to 72 hours. Only then did I go to the Y, make dinner and hope for a good night's sleep. I was proud of myself for being persistent, forceful and outraged in ways that were more like the old ME than me.

My notes about the next day, Friday the 15th, started, "Let me be a journalist here and start with the headline: ME staying put at SKNRC." Then I detailed a long day filled with chores, phone calls, red tape, uncertainty and one major decision. At the end of the day, the appeal dragged on and was beginning to feel like a comedy of errors unacknowledged by the company supposedly managing it. The decision that SKNRC would be ME's new "home" came when I acknowledged that she could not return to WV, even with additional physical therapy.

WV's nursing director and J had visited ME to assess her ability to return to memory care. They judged that would not be a safe environment for her. I learned of that in a conference call with them and the administrator. It was not what I wanted to hear, but I wasn't surprised. Those three could not have been kinder in delivering the difficult news. It helped me that the administrator, who I respected from our first meeting, spoke positively about SKNRC. But it was J's observations about what she had experienced during the visit that were most useful. She was able to frame things in terms of ME's world, which she described as very small and getting smaller as her disease progressed. J said she had found ME to be content, without anxiety, looking at a book I had left with her. "It is counterintuitive," she said, "but because of the disease she is more free with less freedom" — being in the wheelchair. And that was that. I had paid to keep her apartment for September, so I had until the end of the month to clear it out.

I immediately called Mike to fill him in, and that conversation also helped quell my uneasiness. He said he and Caryl had talked after their first visit with ME about how they were pleasantly and positively surprised by SKNRC, and how content ME seemed there. Most important, he was "totally onboard" with my decision. When I hung up, I was at peace with the decision, too. It really had been made with ME's best interests in mind. I recognized that my discomforts with the nursing home (finally I could call it that) were about me, and that I was becoming more comfortable as

I became more familiar with it, the staff and the routines. Thus it was that when I went to visit, I took the checkbook and paid for the rest of September. I returned home to more bureaucracy, yet another demand from the appeals company. What a mess, I thought, but I had no choice except to continue to pursue it.

Saturday I played "appeal phone tag." Maddening. In the midst of the craziness, however, I sensed a change in myself. During my visit with ME, we sat in the Activities Room during a sing-along. She participated some, as did I — a first. Later I wrote:

> I think I have come to see how I was holding on to hope about ME's being able to return to WV, and now realize that because of her disease she doesn't know the difference. When I feel bad about where she is, I need to realize that is *my* issue. When I put her safety and well-being front and center, clearly she is at a point in this journey where she needs a higher level of care. And now she is getting it.

I also realized that I was stronger than I gave myself credit for. "And more loving. Every visit is grounded in love, made possible by her time at WV and my time recharging. I can offer her a tenderness that was absent for months and months. We both can move forward."

For me, the first significant step forward was emptying ME's apartment. I finally said goodbye to WV on September 18. I choked back tears as I talked one last time with J. I left a box of candy for the staff, with a handwritten note expressing our gratitude for their care and many kindnesses. That day was also the first in three weeks that I did not see ME. I needed to be sad alone. I again was in mourning, although not as profoundly as in June.

And, believe it or not, I was still fighting with Medicare. On September 19, a Tuesday, I finally reached a person, and after almost two hours on the phone — much of it on hold — I got ME's appeal filed. Thank goodness I had kept meticulous notes and a timeline of calls, messages and *their* missed deadlines. After all the hiccups, I was not optimistic, but I was proud of myself for persevering on her behalf. On Saturday the 23rd, I was told the appeal had been approved, which meant more skilled-care coverage for ME. I was elated. My celebration was premature. I got another call, this one saying the appeal was being sent off for a second-level appeal because the company managing it had missed a deadline. When I asked about the previous call, I was told the error had been discovered after it was made. What incompetence!

In the midst of this battle, I was in Wisconsin for my much-anticipated Sisters Week. I found myself in need of a piece of information about ME that I did not have, so I called PondView, hoping the nurse I had come to depend on could help me. She did, but not before she told me a story that had me laughing uproariously. Turned out that the unit's Casanova had gotten down on one knee and proposed to ME. That upset his "girlfriend," another resident. ME was oblivious to it all, the nurse said.

For the second-level appeal, I once more provided the necessary information, and lo and behold, before I left Wisconsin I was told that a letter was in the mail allowing ME 12 days of additional coverage. It wasn't much, but it was something. Victory. Nightmare over! I was reminded of what I used to tell my journalism students: All they can do is say "no," but they can't even say that if you don't ask. I had to ask again and again, but in the end ME — and her checkbook — was the better for it.

Back in Rhode Island, my life settled into its new rhythm, one bordering on the slightly comfortable. Sleep continued to be an issue. It was weird that whenever I awoke in the night, there first would be a song playing in my head, then the ruminating would begin. (To this day, that happens more often than not.) The house was too quiet; I missed that "other heart beating." Some days I was almost manic about completing tasks; other days I felt worn out. I continued to visit ME almost daily. She enjoyed my treats — ice cream, chocolate kisses, cookies, now and then fresh fruit. I could make her laugh, which made my heart smile. She was calm. She became adept at getting around in the wheelchair and was social with others. She continued to enjoy live music and sing-alongs. When the fall weather cooperated, I took her outdoors to enjoy fresh air. She seemed content.

I got away for my annual three-night stay in Maine, accompanied by my longtime friend Luise. Her weeklong visit was good for me; our long talks allowed an unburdening like no other. It also taught me that I was comfortable in my house alone, where I was rediscovering how I liked to be. I began to realize how much of myself I had set aside, first in the accommodations that are required of living with love, and then in being a caregiver. I had lots to re-learn about myself.

Sometime in the early morning of October 26, I realized it was exactly four months since I had taken ME to memory care. I did not feel a need to relive that, but I wrote that I did "want to acknowledge that passage of time, all that has happened and changed, and see how I have moved forward. More than baby steps, though probably not yet strides. Certainly there has been some of the proverbial two steps forward, one step back. Indeed, maybe even two or three steps back. But we are at today, and that is what is important." I shared that passage with my therapist later in the day and concluded, "It is good to know that I am OK."

Not only was I OK, but I was determined to make the upcoming holidays my own. Libby and John had invited me to Hilton Head for Thanksgiving. I knew I would miss being with ME and would miss being with our Connecticut family, but I needed to be somewhere different this year, so I said yes. Time with friends, in my favorite place, would be a step forward. And it was.

Whenever I was away, I could not help but wonder if this would be the return when ME no longer recognized me. After Thanksgiving, then, I was relieved that she knew me, although she did not have much attention span for visiting. There was no indication that she in any way realized she had not seen me in nine days. I brought her a slice of Key lime pound cake, which did not spark any recognition. Honestly, I think she would have preferred ice cream.

An even bigger step forward for me was Christmas in northern Virginia with my nephew and his family. After several Decembers with little joy, the thrill of Christmas morning in the company of three young boys was beyond measure. A week without obligations, with others lovingly looking after me, left little time for sadness over being apart from ME for the first Christmas in at least 20 years.

Before I left for Virginia, I had been reading a book whose themes of resilience and love resonated with me. Resilience — my own and ME's — prompted me to write again, after a few weeks of silence. I thought about how ME had adjusted to SKNRC; indeed, as I wrote Christmas cards for her and shared news of her circumstances, over and over I wrote, "She has adjusted remarkably well." That was validated for me at her three-month care-planning meeting. I had validation of my own evolving adjustment from my sessions with Beverly, from regular conversations with friends. "And it comes from within, as I acknowledge progress in moving forward, and from my actions, such as being at peace with a choice to do or not do something, to visit or not visit ME."

In the safe space I share with my therapist, I wrote, "I have been able to say aloud how long it was that I did not feel love for ME but only a sense of obligation. How long it was that I could not bring myself to say, 'I love you.' How long it was that I seldom kissed her, or hugged her, or even touched her in any kind of affectionate way. And how good it feels to NOT be in that place anymore. That is the gift SKNRC has given me, and before that WV. Space and time to rediscover love, which I now share freely." Although indirectly, I characterized ME's dementia as the source of a gift I had been given. It would be some time before that idea blossomed.

"[T]his loss . . . does not go away. My imagined future is gone. It changed me. It changed my life. Now I have to find new possibilities, a new beginning that wakes up the forgotten parts of me, the pieces of me I'd set aside."

The Bookshop at Water's End
Patti Callahan Henry

CHAPTER 9

Rediscovering Me

The "long goodbye" is used often to describe how dementia is experienced by caregivers and others. As I looked back on the time following ME's move to the nursing home, I began to see that as my "long hello."

Reflecting on her life, actress Annette Bening observed in an interview that "a lot of women have a period of incredible growth after their children are no longer with them on a day-to-day basis." I think the same can be said of many individuals after they are freed from 24/7 caregiving. The reclaiming of one's life, I realized, need not wait for the death of the person being cared for!

The more of my notes and emails I read, the more I saw myself reemerging. It was a metamorphosis from caregiver to me, both my essential being and new ways of being. That journey was not easy, was not without pain, was not without starts and stops, was not short. That journey, I hope, never will be complete.

I cannot pinpoint exactly when that journey began, so I choose to start this description of it with me back on the roller coaster. It was 6:55 a.m.

on December 30, 2017, and I had just gotten off the phone with the PondView nurse. ME had experienced a short seizure about 3 a.m.; the CNA got to her just as it was ending. The nurse said the seizure surprised everyone. She reported that ME was "back to her normal self," but was tired and a bit pale. The doctor ordered bloodwork and suggested obtaining permission for a neurological consult. I told the nurse they should do whatever was needed. I also asked her to explain a seizure to me. I decided to stick to my plan not to visit that day, allowing ME to rest. I was not sure about that decision, but I am sure I was nervous. I wrote: "If I were superstitious I would be at the point of thinking every time I return from being away, something bad happens. Yikes. But of course it is just the serendipity I am so fond of turned on its head. Sigh."

Another nurse called with an afternoon update, which was they were still waiting on the bloodwork and ME was exhibiting pain in her left hip and knee (her good side). X-rays were ordered. The nurse seemed puzzled by ME's symptoms, but clearly something was going on. About 9:30 I called to see how she was doing. The nurse described her as "feisty." They had finished taking the X-rays and she was not happy. Bloodwork did not show anything and no other tests had been ordered. The doctor was in the building but had not yet made it to PondView. Did I want to be called if they got any results? Only if there is something serious, I said. I hoped to relax, watch a college football game and then sleep. I hoped ME could settle down and also get some rest.

New Year's Eve day was cold, and I had to shovel snow before I visited ME. She was in bed when I got there after lunch. I found her alert, a bit pale. She was on her left side, the one that seemed to be painful. She responded to me affectionately and I got her laughing. I talked with the nurse, who said the X-rays only showed osteoarthritis, which I knew had been diagnosed years ago, and no pneumonia. That's all we would know for now.

By the middle of the afternoon, I was settled in for a New Year's Eve even more quiet than usual. I could not recall the last time I made it to midnight; with each passing year I had less and less interest in merrymaking. "I will be glad to see 2017 go," I wrote, "but I don't have expectations for 2018. Right now I just want to see ME feeling better." As for myself, "I have lived alone for six months now. It is both comfortable and not. Some spaces I have claimed for my own, but in much of the house it is as if I am waiting for ME to return. *Forward resumes tomorrow.* No resolutions, but I will make a list of tasks and begin to tackle them. And I will try to live my life one day at a time."

When the world got back to work on January 2, I visited ME, but not until the middle of the afternoon. I found her in her wheelchair in the main room, which was reassuring. Melissa, a nurse I had come to respect and trust more each day, was on duty. She said ME had been sluggish in the morning and was fed her breakfast, but by lunch she was more like herself and ate well on her own. Everyone I talked with seemed generally happy about that, and perhaps relieved. I brought "Ms. Sweet Tooth" holiday chocolates, which she devoured, and if she seemed a tad subdued she was generally engaged. I left breathing easier. Even easier after a call from the neurological nurse practitioner with whom we had worked for so long. She helped me better understand seizures, how one might cause hip/leg discomfort, how a neurological workup might be of only minimal value, how there was no reason for medication in ME's current circumstance. I told her how thankful I was that she remained available for us.

Then I turned my attention to myself. My calendar no longer revolved around four-hour blocks for care assistants for ME, but around appointments and activities for me. My morning notes were more sporadic. My emails to family and friends began to be more about how I was adjusting and coping (or not), although ME was almost always included. As my "battery" recharged, I committed to saying "yes" more often than "no" to whatever came my way. Giving myself permission to do so took time, no doubt about it. My courage was fostered by my therapist, a steadying presence in my life. There were plenty of constants, too.

Sleep, for example, continued to vex me. For decades, I had been nine- to ten-hour-a-night sound sleeper. That changed significantly with ME's illness and try as I might, I never have "recovered." My notes repeatedly reminded me of that; often they began with an observation like this from early January:

> Tuesday's sleep until 7:30 seems to have been a one and done. Up today at 5:15. Makes for a long Sunday. Was -2 outside, and of course pitch black. Now it 7:30. Clear blue sky, but little warmth in the day ahead. Already I have read a chunk of my Bernie Gunther tale, eaten breakfast, checked emails and FaceBook and played five games of the addictive Hungry Babies. ME's clean clothes are piled on the couch next to me. Later today I will deliver several days' worth and "visit" awhile. I am so relieved that she is "back" from last weekend's seizure. But her attention span continues to shrink and visits are short. . . . I will admit to sometimes being torn, wanting her to have some company but at the same time not wanting to make the effort.

I continued to make the effort for regular visits to the Y. When the fitness room closed for renovations, I surprised myself by checking out our town's new recreation center. In the past, the interruption to my routine likely would have marked its death knell. I was determined not to let that happen, and spent those weeks using the center's walking track — for free! On that Sunday, my plan for me: shower and dress, get to the rec center for a walk during its limited hours, enjoy soup and salad at Panera, do a bit of work — and then see ME. "Will the only conversations be in my head?" I wrote. "I hope not."

In my last chaotic months of direct caregiving, I welcomed silence. Now, with only me in the house, I welcomed sound. I was grateful for conversations. Regular coffee hours with Sandra and lunches with Linda. Regular outings and dinners with Sandra and Roberta. Phone calls with my sister. The one sound I had little interest in was the television. I had thought about "cord cutting" but knew that would be impossible with ME at home. When I did finally cancel cable service, I found that "streaming" changed my viewing habits for the better. I was determined to not allow TV to intrude on my days; I could even ignore it in the evening — now and then. Movies were a different matter. I wasn't shy about taking advantage of Senior Day, didn't mind going to the movie theater alone. Looking back, 2018 was a good year for that.

Every "yes" I offered to an invitation felt like an important step forward. I was taking care of me, but in another respect I was allowing my friends to take care of me, too. I never had been good at that. I think learning that lesson early in my journey out of caregiving was an essential piece of my personal growth.

At the same time, ME remained a focus of most of my days. I knew I was not alone in that regard as I came to recognize the nursing home "regulars." I also was learning to be comfortable with others visiting ME without me. Mike and Caryl were incredibly attentive, making their two-hour drive every couple of weeks. Sometimes I would join them, other times I would not but might meet them afterward for lunch. Those breaks, when I knew ME would have company and it didn't have to be me, were important to my forward momentum.

I had planned to be in Stockbridge, Massachusetts, for my birthday on January 23, but the forecast for snow postponed those plans. Over the years, our Christmas trees often remained decorated long enough to serve as a birthday tree, and this year I had carried on that tradition — albeit with my small artificial Packers tree. That was not enough to keep me from feeling blue, however. "A few cards are under it, waiting to be opened tomorrow," I wrote on the 22nd. "I don't expect any gifts. Painful for someone who, even in adulthood, has loved birthday presents. . . . High winds probably will keep me from going to Newport for lunch. I am sad." I was remembering birthday night in Cusco, Peru, three years before, when I tried a video chat with ME, who did not even know it was my birthday. I was remembering how ME tried so hard with gift giving, wanting to choose something "perfect" and never feeling as if she had. It made me sad that her last gifts to me had been very impersonal — cash. So I hung on to the year (1993; early in our relationship) when she gave me golf clubs, which got me back playing the game I love. I counseled myself that "tomorrow is a day for no expectations!"

When I got up the next morning, I resolved that it was going to be a good birthday, that I would enjoy myself, and that I would do new things. It was. I did. First up was a funny e-card from my oldest nephew and greetings from my middle nephew and his wife, who were in New Zealand.

I was at the Y before 8, then met Sandra for coffee. A beautiful card from her and Roberta along with my only gift. We had a good gab, as usual. Back home, I turned on the birthday tree and opened my cards. There were also several Facebook wishes and more online greetings as the day progressed, along with electronic messages from the likes of my dentist, the Y and an alumni group. Smile.

I did skip Newport and opted instead for lunch at a lovely restaurant near Narragansett Beach, where I could watch the surf from my window-side table. I read as I savored my French onion soup and salad with lobster, not the least bit self-conscious. It was rainy and gusty when I left, and I got soaked on the way to my car. Nonetheless, I headed north to pick up a free slice of cake. Nothing was going to stop me from sharing birthday cake with ME. When I told her it was my birthday, she responded, "It is?!" Beyond that, I am sure it didn't mean anything to her. But sharing that Lemon Burst slice meant everything to me! The residents were just starting a sing-along when I arrived, and I could tell that ME was antsy to join them, so after the cake I wheeled her back to the main room, gave her a kiss, fetched her laundry and left. By then she was eating a cookie. Smile. Back home, the rest of my day was low-key. I turned on the birthday tree, to enjoy it one last time. Texts and Facebook posts continued throughout the evening. And there was a nice call from Mike. I ended No. 69 by writing, "I must never forget how much I am loved."

To keep myself busy that winter, I began the daunting chore of decluttering the study. When ME retired in 2003, she had brought home boxes, bags and files of stuff from her spacious office. We put much of it in the basement, but a lot got piled on the study floor. She promised to deal with it. She never did. Now I wondered if it was because she had been overwhelmed, and if that were a precursor of the brain changes to come. I know I was overwhelmed by the enormity of disposing of her things. But eventually it had become almost impossible to maneuver anywhere in the room except to my desk, so I had no choice. When she first was gone from the house, I had neither emotional nor physical energy to deal with the room I hated to look at. So I kept the door closed. When eventually I opened it, I was also opening a bit more of myself to live in the moment, to claim another room of the house as mine.

It was not easy. I could handle only an hour or so at a time as I unearthed all sorts of memories. I began jotting thoughts as they came to me, "because down the road I am unlikely to recall" my feelings, I noted. I was confident that I knew how ME would have handled items, and I felt a responsibility to do things her way. I might have recycled papers without looking at them, but she would have been chagrined to do that. So I at least glanced at everything, sorted, organized. Before long I had at least 40 pounds to shred and bags and bags to recycle. I agonized over files that might have gone to the university archives, then decided ME had not sent them there so neither would I — a decision that even now gives me pause.

I knew ME had been a saver, but until I got into this project I did not realize how much she had saved — and for how long. Mementos I could understand. Every note, email, invitation, thank-you from family members I could understand. But decades-old bills and bank statements, empty envelopes, holiday cards from a paper carrier etc. etc. — these I could not understand. At times I felt like a snoop, but I had to check every envelope and glance at its contents, just in case I might find something tucked away.

Which did happen now and then. To avoid "rabbit holes," I put many items in a "second sort needed" pile; it didn't take long for me to have a tower.

I set aside a few books for family members, but saved three room-high bookcases for later. I opened the four drawers of a dresser; two were filled with socks! I decided the dresser could wait. So could the room-length closet, stuffed floor to ceiling. By mid-February, I was working on another book editing project, so it was rewarding to sit at my computer and slowly begin to see progress around the room. Of course, the guest room next door had become my "holding pen," and soon that was the door I kept closed.

Not surprisingly, whenever I made decisions about ME's belongings I had to confront my own feelings. Sometimes I was angry with her for not doing what she had promised when she retired. Sometimes I felt sad; love oozed out of all those family items. Sometimes I was painfully reminded of what dementia had stolen from her. Oftentimes I just had to take a deep breath and remember how well she had adjusted to her new environment. "Everyone communicates to me that she is doing 'excellent,' I wrote to J from memory care after she visited ME. "The disease progresses, of course. She is quieter, but still loves her sweets! Her empathy for other residents has impressed the staff." Knowing those things helped me let go of what she had not been able to.

The February 7 note I wrote late in the day reflected my immersion in memories. On my drive to Providence for a therapy session, I wrote, "I was mulling over what to address" and realized how much I had been thinking about memories and memory. "Blame it not just on the circumstances of my life at the moment, but also the book I just finished (*The Bastard of*

Istanbul), my recent birthday, et al." I scribbled the beginning of a poem, "which came to me in a torrent"

> I am the repository of your memories
>
> Your stories
>
> Your history
>
> Your hopes
>
> Your dreams.
>
> I did not ask for this responsibility.
>
> Your damn disease gave it to me.
>
> The damn disease that is wiping clean your slate
>
> Has me filling in the blanks for you
>
> Preserving . . . .

This was six months into ME living at SKNRC, and I continued to adjust to the nursing home. A few times I did have to correct someone who assumed I was ME's daughter. The first time I said "no, her partner," I felt uncomfortable. The next time was easier. And if I felt saying that might be problematic, I would simply say "no, her friend." The more staff and I got to know one another, the more I realized our relationship was not an issue. I believed they saw how much I loved ME and how attentive I was to her needs. So I didn't think twice about choosing to take part in the Valentine's Day luncheon. I look at a photo from it and my heart smiles. In an email to Jane, I described it this way: "The Valentine's lunch was VERY nice. There were five twosomes, off in the 'quiet' room. Tables decorated. Staff waited on us. Got a bottle of sparkling grape juice, shrimp cocktail with four giant shrimp, prime rib, fingerling potatoes and squash, with cheesecake with strawberries for dessert. Everything was tasty. And leisurely. Frankly, was nicest Valentine's Day in several years." The

Activities staff could not have done more to make us feel special.

I also shared the photo with Jane, writing that "you may notice ME is without her glasses. They seem to have disappeared. Ordered her a new pair yesterday. Also note that she is not wearing red, despite the fact that I made sure there were two red tops in her closet. Oh well, I no longer sweat the small stuff. Yay me."

It was only somewhat true that I no longer fretted about things such as clothing choices, missing personal items or laundry issues. Indeed, I remember apologizing to Sandra more than once for spending so much of our coffee time on such concerns. To my therapist, I often concluded a rant by saying, "I know it shouldn't matter so much . . . ." What was really going on, I know now, is that I thought I knew better how things "should" be done. That had been going on since I moved her to memory care. "Who will know that you like your sandwich cut in quarters?" I mused the day I left her at WV. Over time, it turned out, the more I found me, the easier it was to let go and allow the professionals to do their jobs. And the more I did that, the more of me I found.

As I became increasingly comfortable with ME's care, my visits became shorter and a tad less frequent. That was good for my mental health, and thankfully she did not seem to realize how much time passed between them. In late February, I wrote my uncle that I would be traveling for two weeks in mid-March and 10 days in April. I said I thought those would be good "tests" of my growing resolve to take care of me. I wrote him while I waited on Linda to arrive from Providence. We were finally heading to Stockbridge — Norman Rockwell territory — for two nights at the historic Red Lion Inn. (Our travel jinxes continued; these plans had been delayed three times by weather!) That trip tested me in another way. We went to nearby Pittsfield, ME's hometown, to visit a museum. I am not a cemetery person, but I could not be in the city without also visiting the family graves on ME's behalf. My fingers were crossed that entire stop because I had not alerted her brother that I would be in town. ME probably didn't realize his absence from her life, but I did.

I passed the "tests" of longer periods away — in a couple ways. Similar to a year earlier, snow threatened my early March trip to California. The "new" me didn't wait for the airline to change my plans; I proactively changed them (cost me some money, but what the hell). My sister and I got there, handled our kid-sitting duties, enjoyed lots of family time, some poolside sun, a Pacific coast beach and more. My immune system still was weary from caregiving, however, and I caught a misery-inducing cold/sinus thing the kids had when we arrived. Every time someone went to a store, I asked for another box of tissues. I also put my back out just as we were leaving for the airport and our return flights. But . . . ME was *not* constantly at the forefront of my thoughts and I called only a couple times to check on her. When I needed to, I could talk about her, but I didn't need to nearly as much.

My April trip was to Hilton Head. The fact that I have no notes from it, and found only passing mentions in emails, says it all, I think: It was an ordinary vacation. The fact that I stopped to see ME on my way home from the airport was "routine." And I was feeling good about plans Kris and I had begun discussing in earnest — New Zealand in November (an early celebration of my 70th birthday) and Florida January through March. A year earlier, even thinking about such plans would have been folly.

I had been pondering ME's May 30 birthday for some time. I desperately wanted it to be better than her last at home. I wanted to do something special while she was able to enjoy it. I brainstormed ideas until the perfect one came to me on a drive to the nursing home: an "ice cream social" for all of PondView — residents and staff. There was no disputing that ME's favorite treat was ice cream, in particular that from our local shop. The owners were our former neighbors, and I was able to arrange for them to deliver make-your-own sundaes. It was a grand day. Mike, Caryl, a couple nieces and some "grands," along with Sandra and Roberta and numerous residents, joined us. We were able to be on the sun porch. ME loved being the center of attention, responded to the love that enveloped her — and was so social that her sundae melted before she could eat all of it. The day was all about ME, which is the way I wanted it. I had been nervous about pulling it off, but as I told everyone, "It could not have gone better!" A year earlier I could not have imagined such a feat.

Change is seldom easy. For those in the throes of caregiving, personal change may not even be on the radar screen. I know it had not been for me. I know that for years, I could not imagine a time when I might come and go as I pleased. I could not imagine life without daily drama. I could not imagine my world expanding rather than contracting. I could not imagine ME finding peace living in a nursing home. I could not imagine me being at peace with ME living in a nursing home. Yet that is what had happened. When that peace was disturbed, it was either because of illness or my discomfort with a change to ME's routine.

I was fond of saying that "we didn't choose SKNRC, it was chosen for us" after ME was initially admitted for rehabilitation following hip surgery. As luck would have it, she was the second person in her room and so didn't get the window bed. When that room was to be renovated, she was moved to another corridor, in a bright room with two windows. I liked everything about that for her, if I overlooked the little man who was fond of rifling through her closet. On June 1, I got a letter informing me that some rooms — including ME's — were being converted to singles. I was not happy, but it would not have been economically responsible to pay the higher rate. That meant she would be moved again.

Because I liked her aides, I wrote the administrator that "I trust the folks on PondView who work with her regularly can assist in figuring out the best spot for her." I did ask if she could get a window bed. As luck would have it, she ended up back in her original room, nicely renovated, and this time she had the window. I quickly came to appreciate that a dozen fewer residents made the unit much quieter. I also noticed that her things didn't disappear any more. It was almost a year since ME had left home, and I felt she was finally settled.

Every day I was more settled, too, and more able to deal with the occasional unsettling moment. I finally decided, for example, to cancel the land line and use only my cell phone. As much as it pained me each month to pay Verizon, I had not been able to bring myself to give up the number that ME had had since she moved to Rhode Island in 1973. When I shed that sentimentality, I took another step forward. "I might be slow to the party," I wrote my nephew Bill after he congratulated me for canceling, "but eventually I get there."

I was confident that eventually I would get through all the "firsts" since ME no longer was at home. But June was a difficult month; try as I might I could not seem to keep from anticipating the last "first" — the day I drove her to memory care. I found myself writing frequent notes again:

June 19 — I am not intentionally thinking about a year ago, but [it] seems never far from my mind. Perhaps that accounts for the return to early waking. I no longer am escaping, however. I greet each day with thanks, and I face most days with energy and resolve. . . . Last week I said to [my therapist] that I honestly do not know where the year has gone. It seems now to have passed with the speed of light. Could I have ever imagined bouncing into SKNRC with fragrant peonies for ME and going from person to person so each could smell them?! Did I think I would rediscover my love for ME, not just a sense of responsibility for her?! Did I believe I could be happy again?! Did I believe ME could be calm again, absent anger, anxiety and frustration?! I don't need to look back at my notes from those months leading up to moving her to memory care. They are as vivid to me as yesterday. Which is why I can see how that BIG decision has, ultimately, given us each a life that can be lived and not just endured. My goal is to make the most of each day. ME is always in my day, even when I do not see her. She is safe and cared for and loved. I can ask for no more.

June 20 — I really hope that when I emerge on the other side of this "year ago" period I can find a way to sleep a bit longer into the early morning. Until that happens, however, I try to make the best of things. Coffee. Disarm the new [security] system. Open the blinds. Greet the world — aloud — with thanks for the day and for yesterday, with thanks for at least three things, with a wish for the day, and always ending, "Watch over ME, keep her safe and healthy, bring her peace, a bit of joy, and let her know how very much I love her."

Tomorrow summer arrives officially. Today I plan some serious weeding, an early lunch with Linda, a few groceries so I can make a decent dinner, time with ME, perhaps more yard work. My evenings have a sameness, which sometimes feels boring and other times comforting. I have adapted to no cable, thus no Red Sox, and generally don't miss either. Netflix binging suits me — for the time being, at least. So does reading *The New York Times* in late afternoon/early evening — on the porch the last couple of days. I am so glad I set it up.

There is so much I miss about ME. Time together on the porch, relaxing with good books, the Red Sox on hot summer evenings — [these are] in the forefront now. I miss our drives. I miss finding any excuse to go to Westerly, which meant an excuse to get Dairy Queen. I am so glad that as her disease progressed, but was not yet debilitating, I found adventures for us to share. Facebook periodically reminds me of one of them. Who knew an algorithm could spark such feeling?

June 26 — Nothing like getting up at 5 a.m. and discovering you don't have water to block "anniversary" memories! I methodically went downstairs, used bottled water to take my Synthroid, checked the basement for water, hoping upon hope that there would be none. There wasn't. Fetched another bottle and made a cup of coffee. Just as I opened the blinds in the den, a water company truck circled the cul-de-sac, and I thought to myself, "good sign." I also looked up their emergency number so I could report the outage. Learned there is a break somewhere and they are looking for it. And so I picked up my routine . . . . AND said to myself, "You can do this." About then, I remembered what/how a year ago was. And I am OK. Indeed, in the midst of reading I said aloud about myself, *"This was the moment when she realized she would be OK."*

I already have acknowledged the passing of the year in a positive way: I wrote notes of gratitude to Libby and John, Sandra and Roberta, Mike and Caryl, and Jane. The people, along with my family (and my therapist, of course), who have been — and continue to be — my rocks. I see Beverly tomorrow, but I think we can focus on the here and now, not the year gone by. And who would have thought that was possible when I was in the throes of upheaval?!

What I found different in myself was I now knew enough to allow myself to feel — sad, scared, relieved, hopeful . . . whatever. I did not hide from my feelings; if anything, I overcompensated by doing. My friend Linda and I had taken another road trip, this time to Hyde Park, New York, where she had spent so much time researching a book. I never had been to that area, so we did a lot of tourist things. It was fabulous, as was my favorite souvenir: a hardcover copy of *Eleanor and Hick* I bought at the Val-Kill gift shop for $10.

Once home, I tackled house projects that had been deferred by ME's illness. I had a security system installed. Not because I was afraid, but to feel secure when I traveled without burdening neighbors. I got the driveway sealed. I did yard work and began garden maintenance that had been neglected for two years or more. I also worked on a book for two academics who hired me to format it for self-publishing. Eventually they asked if I would edit it, which I did (having underpriced my time yet again). They chose a publisher that was new to me, and it turned out, after I had designed and formatted the book's interior, the publisher could not use my work. So finally I told the authors it was in their best interest to contract with a designer. I was disappointed, but also told myself not to accept another project until fall. It was during all that activity I decided to write those gratitude notes — hand-written and personalized. In saying thank you, I was able to let go of the past year.

Well, not quite. There remained the not-insignificant task of preparing my first annual status report and financial accounting for the Probate Court, which proved much more time-consuming than I anticipated. Navigating bureaucracy is never easy. When I finally found the forms I needed, I was flummoxed by what went where for the financial accounting. (I subsequently deduced that lawyers or accountants usually do this.) Once my lawyer explained how that accounting worked, I was off to the races. I never have been afraid of numbers. I balanced ME's checkbooks monthly. I kept meticulous records on every penny I spent on her behalf. I kept every bank statement, investment report, tax document and more. Nonetheless, getting every dollar in the right place required a lot of pencil lead and erasing, calculating and recalculating — until I was comfortable with an "accounting adjustment" less than $100.

Thankfully, before I even started on that chore I spent two weeks in Wisconsin, enjoying what felt like my first real vacation in years. My phone rang only once, and that was a robocall. Jane had recently observed, "I am sure that you are still adjusting to all the changes and will continue to for some time. It is time that you start taking care of yourself and really putting yourself first." The day before I left for Wisconsin, I had written to tell her all that I planned and noted, "I can honestly say that I am taking good care of me and moving forward. . . . I am able to [make this trip] with only a bit of trepidation and a whole lot of eagerness."

Jane also had commented on my continued devotion to ME. "To this day, you are still caring for [her] and making sure her needs are met. I have to smile every time I see a picture of the two of you. I wonder what ME is thinking and what she is feeling, and does she even know how wonderful you are making her life, as limited as her life is at this point. To say that [she] is one lucky person is an understatement." As I saw it, I also was one lucky person, not the least because I could ensure her "presence" at family (hers and mine) gatherings.

I told Jane about my trip to Connecticut for our oldest grand-niece's high school graduation party. "I sure don't know where those years have gone. Seems like just yesterday ME and I saw her at two days old!" Remembering that was bittersweet. A couple of times when ME had been ill (and certain she was dying), she told me that all she wanted was "to see the kids grow up." As I wrote to Jane, "It is sad that she is missing their milestones, but I bring her in my heart when I can be present for them." And that is why there was no way that I would miss Mike and Caryl's 50th anniversary bash the weekend after I returned from Wisconsin.

It was one of those drive-two-hours, stay-two-hours, drive-two-hours trips. Time with our Connecticut family is as important to me as time with my family. My latest trip to Wisconsin again had proved to me that I could confidently go away. My time at the anniversary party helped me see that I functioned as a "single" in healthy ways. For example, I was chatting with two widows and learned that neither would go to restaurants alone. One put it this way: "I hate it when they call my name and say 'table for one'." I don't think they believed me when I told them I often eat out alone. That I always have a book and am not the least bit reluctant to read it during my meal.

I also think it is healthy that I enjoy my own company. No doubt my situation was different from theirs, because I still had my partner in my life. But my house had just one beating heart, as did theirs. The more I learned to not have expectations about ME, but to accept "who" I found when I visited, the more rewarding our time together was. That made the empty house and silences manageable. After all, if I could enjoy the ME of the moment, I could enjoy the me of the moment, too.

Of course, just when I thought I had taken another step forward in my journey, ME's dementia would show me that might not be true. More than once I wondered whether I was "cursed or blessed." For example, when I walked in the door from my Wisconsin trip, the smoke detector was chirping, signaling it needed a new battery. I felt cursed. I found the instructions. Oh no, I had saved the Spanish version! Thank goodness for the internet. Oh no, the instructions stated that I needed a professional to change the battery. They did, however, provide steps to temporarily silence the chirping. Oh no, that didn't work. All I could do was hope the chirping had started days earlier, because the instructions said it only would continue for about a week.

That night, I slept pretty well once I discovered that a pillow wrapped around my head dulled the incessant, annoying chirp. In the morning, when I checked my phone it showed a call and voicemail from the nursing home. Why hadn't I heard it ring? ME had had a 90-second seizure. The nurse, who had been on duty seven months before when she had her first episode, said this one was different. Tests had been ordered. Reassuringly, she said ME was sitting at a table and having her juice. "She will probably have a better day than I will," the nurse quipped. I felt blessed to have enjoyed my vacation before this latest "crisis," and a bit cursed that it occurred on the heels of my return. But, I wrote in my morning note, "I am trying to handle the reality, not conjecture. One step at a time. And I will visit and bring ice cream as promised."

I was still feeling blessed the next morning after I got a text from Caryl saying she and Mike were on their way home from Cape Cod and were going to visit ME. I told her about the seizure and said I would meet them at the nursing home mid-afternoon. There, we chatted about an hour; ME was a bit lethargic but looked good. She even rolled her eyes and laughed at me as I fed her ice cream, which amused Mike. I also felt blessed to have dinner plans that evening with Roberta and Sandra, including ice cream of our own for dessert. Blessed to have air conditioning to go home to. Blessed to sleep until 6:15 a.m. Monday.

A week or so later, I still was feeling more blessed than cursed. (I had convinced an electrician to disconnect the smoke detectors because my security system now monitored that. It took him less than 10 minutes. I was appalled that he charged me $125.) One of the nurses had suggested that ME could get palliative care, and after a gulp and a deep breath, I saw the value in that. Palliative care proved to be a long-lasting blessing for ME — and me. I also was preparing for a visit from my nephew and family. Indeed a blessing for me.

Adding five (including boys 10, 7 and 4) to my household for ten days was hectic, at times chaotic, always FUN. The itinerary one day, for example, was: bacon and eggs for six; exploring Beavertail State Park; a picnic lunch at Fort Weatherill State Park; a stop at a Jamestown playground; ice cream at Brickley's; hanging out and talking on the screened-in porch; and movie night with a giant bowl of Peruvian popcorn. I enjoyed sharing my early mornings, when the older two would join me for reading in the den-turned-my-bedroom. I loved that the oldest and I were able to sneak out very early one morning to get "special" donuts. I smiled with every loving hug from the youngest. I cleverly paid the boys a penny for each Rose of Sharon bloom they picked up from the driveway and front yard. There were thousands!

I wanted to show off as much of Rhode Island as possible. We spent one day in Newport. At Fort Adams, which dates to 1799, we explored inside the fort without paying for a tour, thanks to a nice guy "guarding" the gate as Jazz Festival preparations were under way. Then we went to Brenton Point for a picnic. Kite flying took a bit of doing, and they ended up buying a basic one (what a great idea to have a "kite truck"). I also treated us all to another Rhode Island classic, Del's frozen lemonade. That night, Bill made individual pizzas for supper, then we went to downtown Wakefield for RiverFire. We walked the length of Main Street, stopping for ice cream at the apothecary's old-fashioned soda fountain. Rose of Sharon money burning holes in their pockets, the boys were allowed to shop at Main Street Candy on the way back to the car. Whew!

If that day wore me out, my company seemed indefatigable. Their day at the beach and another at Mystic Seaport gave me welcome time to recharge. I had a "honey do" list for Bill, who insisted on ticking off the items despite the heat and the humidity. And Shelly had a knack for finding something new for the boys. So "chore day" started with us all in their van for a trip to Home Depot and Best Buy. Shelly had found the Impossible Dream playground, where she and the boys hung out while I spent money (including a long-desired new television for downstairs). We stopped to buy flowers for ME before visiting her on the way home. She seemed to especially enjoy the boys. Once home, Bill cleaned my lower rain gutters and repaired several, then trimmed some bushes. Connor wasn't feeling well, so we got take-out Thai for Shelly and Xavier, and warmed leftovers for Max. Bill and I went to Matunuck Oyster Bar. Well-fed, we started the TV swap, only possible because Bill and Shelly could carry the heavy, heat-producing plasma upstairs. I was one happy camper. One blessed aunt. When, after nine days vacationing with me they left for home, I was glad to reclaim my space, peace and quiet — and within an hour already missed them.

Ten days later I brought Jane up to date: "Things here are good. As I said to my therapist a couple weeks ago, I am content. What an amazing realization. After having my nephew and his family here . . . I also realized I miss daily interactions and everyday conversation about matters big and small. But I also like my quiet and my space."

I also described how ME continued to do well. "Can you believe she has been at the nursing home almost a year?" I asked, adding that she was off all her blood pressure meds, and anxiety meds had been cut in half. "Staff thinks she is a bit more alert. I find that to be true sometimes, and other times not. Still loves her sweets."

The summer, one of our hottest on record, wound down. During one stretch, I did not turn off my air conditioning for three weeks, and each day I was thankful that installing it had been the first major decision I made after moving ME to memory care. At the time, I didn't attach any significance to that beyond creature comfort. Now, I see it as my first declaration of independence. I took care of me and because I had, being inside during the heat and humidity was not a problem. Indeed, it allowed me to make significant progress on dealing with decades of photographs, most taken by ME.

That project put my organizational skills to the test. I wasn't sure what I would do with the photos, so I decided to start by sorting them. Luckily, ME had labeled many of the envelopes with the year and events. When I found myself needing help with a date, one look at a photo generally opened my floodgate of memories. Thankfully I was emotionally ready for that. In fact, I enjoyed remembering the people and places, events and celebrations, vacations and more. An idea for a Christmas project took hold. I would do a second version of the "book" of her mother's poems I had made for my first Christmas with ME. This one would match a photograph taken by ME with each poem.

Once I get started on a creative project, I live it, to the exclusion of almost everything else. That was my state of mind on Labor Day weekend. It was my body that reminded me that the holiday also marked an "anniversary," I observed in my morning note. "What I mean is that I have been even more filled with energy, especially early in the day but continuing into the late afternoon. Sleeping but weird dreams, too — the latter is rare." I then summarized the events that started with the early morning phone call about ME being found on the floor, head bleeding. "And our journey to SKNRC was under way. I did not realize it at the time, of course. Certainly I was not prepared for it. But it has been OUR journey. And it continues. I can't know what today holds, or the next, or the next. I do know that I love ME and am here for her/with her." And I knew, too, how grateful I was that she was safe and well cared for. "That gratitude is a gift!"

Now and again, I missed ME so profoundly I felt it with my entire being. It hurt! One late September Sunday was like that. It was a gorgeous fall day, blue sky, sunny, 70 degrees. After breakfast I gardened for two hours, mostly digging out iris and day lilies. I read the newspaper on the porch until lunch, later watched an NFL pregame show. Unexpectedly, restlessness overtook me. I remembered how a couple years ago this was the sort of afternoon where ME and I would have taken a drive to Westerly, gotten DQ, then meandered home on our "scenic route." I realized I had not gone that way since the day before she went to memory care — 15 months ago. I felt sad. Felt the need to get out and do the drive. I wavered. Checked the Weight Watchers point value of a mini Blizzard, then decided it did not matter. This was something I *needed* to do. And so I did.

I enjoyed the warmth inside the car, window down, Fifties music playing. I remembered how much we enjoyed our drives, how it was one thing that calmed ME in the last months. When I got my Blizzard, I "toasted" ME, said aloud how much I missed her. And by the time I got home, the afternoon had wound down and the sadness had returned — more or less — to its hiding place. I had learned to own the feeling, give voice to it, allow it to be. Yay me! I would put that newfound equanimity to the test in the months ahead, particularly with my decision to leave Rhode Island for the winter. The weeks leading up to that trip reinforced for me that I was up to the time away.

For one thing, I was living my life more mindfully than ever. That was my self-assessment after a round of golf. I had gone to bed with a plan for playing early the next day. When I woke to windy conditions, I contemplated not going. But I decided that I could learn something about playing in the wind, so I headed out about 7:30. It looked as if I would play alone, which never bothers me. But at the last minute the starter asked if I minded two "old guys" joining me. "They are fun to play with," he said. So it was nine holes with Ray and Ollie, and Pete (joining us at the fifth hole). I kept thinking that it was like being with a comedy team, Ray and Ollie so obviously enjoying themselves — and playing with me, I think. At one point I overhead them remark, "She plays well." I am proud that I know the rules, know the etiquette, can banter and keep up. I was *soooo* glad I had decided to take the chance to play.

My fall trip to Maine was more mindful, too. I purposely chose different restaurants and savored every bite (Weight Watchers friendly or not). When, relaxing on a waterside bench in Perkins Cove, I overheard a discussion clearly between a daughter and her mother with dementia, I moved. "I don't need this," I thought to myself. I planned a visit to Portland, including stores I had read about in a *New York Times* story, then decided I would enjoy the Art Museum more. Directionally challenged, I had written a route but decided to try my maps app. It worked and I got around quite nicely. I chose a parking garage just down the street from the museum and found a spot near the entrance. So my dislike of such structures and my fear of not finding my car in them proved moot. After lunch, my drive to Twin Lights State Park was pretty, but the park itself felt too empty for me to walk about alone. My next goal was the Prouts Neck area where Winslow Homer had painted. It was a disappointment, with too many private roads and no way to see Homer's vistas. Sigh. But it was important that I had tried!

At the end of the day, I wrote: "I am so proud of myself for going out and about and finding new places to explore. And enjoying myself. Was definitely in the moment today, not in the years of memories made here with ME." The next day was equally filled with me doing things for me. I had read a short interview with a chef in a tourism newspaper. The last question was what one dish he would urge diners to choose, and he had me at "the Bolognese." I took a chance, went there for lunch and savored every scrumptious bite. Later, I was able to sit outside and read without dwelling on a voicemail from the hairdresser at the nursing home. She had been unable to cut ME's hair, she said, because ME had fallen asleep after breakfast and had been in bed since. There was a time when that would have sent me into a worry spin, but on this day it did not. I was content.

Because I would leave Rhode Island before Christmas, I wanted to share Thanksgiving dinner with ME. Then I planned to drive to Connecticut for another meal and an overnight. ME, by this time, was off all meds except for Synthroid and the two drugs that "may be" slowing progression of the disease, but that was unknowable. Some days she napped, but more often than not she didn't. (I finally had learned that my request she not be put in bed was ill-advised and I was happy to let the staff decide what was best for her.) Some days she was more alert and engaged than others. She still laughed, and every now and then said something totally appropriate. Thanksgiving turned out to be a good day — for each of us.

Much of my time after that was devoted to getting the house and me ready for my extended absence. I was constantly making lists, checking them twice. I would fly to Virginia on the 21st, so I had my golf clubs, Christmas gifts and boxes of Florida clothes and necessities shipped there. I would travel with my cold-weather clothes, then swap before we drove south. It seemed more complicated, and expensive, than I anticipated. I managed. "Whatever it takes to make this happen," I thought. That included me asking Sandra to visit the house regularly and try to keep my few plants alive; arranging to have the driveway shoveled when needed; leaving a key and garage door opener with a neighbor; and other such details.

I was delighted when Sandra and Roberta invited me for dinner on the 20th, to celebrate the holidays and Roberta's birthday. "By then I expect to have a house mostly devoid of food," I said in accepting. I also was on the Probate Court docket for that afternoon, to get approval for my annual report. Going to court still made me nervous, "So I will be ready for time with friends," I added. As couples, we four had celebrated together for decades, and exchanged gifts. I reminded Sandra that we had agreed on no gifts. "Your visiting ME is all I want, anyway."

On December 9, a Sunday, I woke up with this mantra running through my head: You will be all right. Which evolved into: I will be OK. You will be OK. We will be OK. "Obviously," I wrote, "I continue to deal with anxiety over going away for 3 1/2 months. I was going to write 'leaving,' but that seems to suggest more permanence. But on this anniversary of Dad's death, I think he was reminding me of what it means to move forward, even after great loss. Mom sure did. And I am." It amused me how often I found myself saying, "You are channeling mom again." When, for example, did I start being cheery and chatty with other residents during my nursing home visits? When did I start singing around the house?

My note continued: "Two weeks from today I will wake up in Fairfax, not to an empty house but to a house of sleeping family. I want to treasure that and each day of this winter's adventure. I don't need to know if it is a one-time thing. I don't need to have a plan. I can be open to saying yes more often than no. I can make progress on figuring out how I want to be at this point in my life. (I started to write 'who' instead of 'how,' but instantly realized I already know WHO I am. And that is a damn grand thing!) So here is a postscript to my morning ritual of greeting the world: Thanks for such insights."

A couple mornings later, I started a new book in William Kent Krueger's Cork O'Connor mystery series, but my mind kept wandering, ruminating on my upcoming leave-taking. Then I read this sentence: "Maybe if he was away from all that was familiar, at least for a while, it might be easier for him to see the path he needed to travel." It struck a chord. I reread it, and then a third time. I put down the book to write a note (uncharacteristically failing to include the book title):

> I guess I am still seeking . . . to make my upcoming Florida stay make some larger sense than just me escaping the cold and snow. Under other circumstances, I don't think that would be necessary. But I seem to need that now. What is the path I am meant to travel moving forward? Or one of the paths? I doubt there is just one. Is it possible that not being alone and in an unfamiliar place (but with the person who has known me the longest) will guide me forward in a way that being here, where past and present cloud a vision of the future, cannot?

Then the afternoon I had been dreading, had fretted about for what felt like forever, arrived. "And you know what," I wrote later, "I am OK, ME is OK, and we are OK! And I have the photos to prove it. I am home after an hour at SKNRC, with some special time giving ME the poems/photos book and an unexpected opportunity to decorate cookies together. I could not have asked for a better visit. And I managed to leave without choking up or breaking down in the car, which has been the picture in my head when I thought about being apart for more than three months. I hugged her, kissed her, and simply said, 'See you later, alligator,' which is how I always leave." I walked to the door without looking back. To take care of me, I wanted only to look forward

". . . much further back I had to face certain difficulties until I decided to accept that . . . a life must be lived as it is. . . . You can not live at all if you do not learn to adapt yourself to your life as it happens to be."

Eleanor Roosevelt
This I Remember
as quoted in *Eleanor and Hick*

CHAPTER 10

Snowbird

I watched the sun rise on 2019 from the back seat of a Dodge Caravan. My sister, brother-in-law and I had left Fairfax at dawn; we hoped to make Jacksonville, Florida, by dark. Winter in Punta Gorda would be the latest milestone in my "long hello" to the me emerging after years of being a caregiver. We three had shared a variety of road-trip adventures in the last several years and created lots of memories. I was confident Florida would be more of the same — a lot more.

The condo that would be our home for three months was owned by my longtime hairdresser, and when it fell into my lap it seemed meant to be. Fred planned to stay a couple weeks, return to Wisconsin until early March, then rejoin us. For two months, it would be Kris and me, living together for the first time in more than 50 years. Later, when we talked about that, each of us admitted to some trepidation. Turned out we meshed easily, and more than once I observed that "Mom and Dad would be so proud of us right now."

Kris did an unbelievable job of driving us around; she was acclimated within a week! In a January 6 email to my friend Sandra, I wrote about the start of our stay: "I just returned from a walk with Kris and finally it is comfy to sit in the lanai. Was 52 when we got up, but is now mid-70s. Not a cloud in the sky. Tomorrow will be more of the same, but warmer. I already am planning on pool time. We have been busy settling in, getting our bearings, getting provisions and shopping for odds and ends that we need/want. . . . We are managing nicely. Also have had several good meals out and last night Kris prepared our own shrimp boil." I did, I added, "have moments where I miss ME and regret that we never were able to do this. Then again, she was probably more like Fred [in that] three weeks away from home would have been her outer limit."

I adapted quickly, which was evident in an email to Jane a week later:

> I have been wanting to respond to your message for some time, but I find that being on Florida time is conducive to thinking "later." Haha. I must say that so far, being a snowbird agrees with me. . . . Kris and I are going to Planet Fitness most mornings and walk most afternoons We found Weight Watchers for my monthly weigh-ins. There is a golf course down the street and I hope to start playing next week. We are going to a Doo-wop tribute concert on Wednesday and have found some other activities.

In those moments when I missed ME, I told Jane, I reminded myself that "I need to live my present life, and I am trying."

In addition to taking advantage of the nearby Planet Fitness. I was committed to the mindful eating ingrained in me by Weight Watchers. So I continued to watch what I ate, but also savored every bite of every slice of Key lime pie and every scoop of ice cream. Kris and I were in sync about exploring the area and choosing concerts, outings and activities that appealed to us. We did so many things I would not have done alone. It was our winter of selfies and Facebook posts. Every photo shows us smiling broadly. Every day extended my "long hello."

After only two weeks, I told Sandra that "every morning I have to talk myself down from calling John to see what he will sell the condo for!" The location suited us; we looked out at Lake Rio ("A 'spit pond' back home in New Hampshire," someone at the pool called it). One sunset was more spectacular than the last. The variety of waterbirds made for great viewing — and photos, as did the 'gator we saw occasionally. With Fred gone, Kris and I did what we wanted when we wanted.

From our first visit, we liked the vibe of Punta Gorda proper, with its walkable downtown and shops. It was a Saturday and we went to check out the weekly farmers market, which became a regular destination — especially for fruit, produce and popcorn. I got hooked on locally roasted coffee (expensive), and Kris and I both were delighted to find a terrific independent bookstore. We identified several restaurants to try. And then there were the murals depicting history and heritage; we saw a few of the 30 that first Saturday and agreed to do the walk/drive tour.

We learned the hard way not to drive to a Gulf Coast beach on a gorgeous Sunday, when parking proved to be non-existent. We settled for lunch and agreed to return on a weekday. We visited historic Englewood, saw a poster for something called Mr. Swindle's Traveling Peculiarium and Drink-ory Garden, and bought tickets as soon as we got home. The Goldtones wowed us with their Doo-wop/oldies performance (we especially appreciated that concerts started at 7). Before our first month ended, we also had visited a botanical and sculpture garden, a funky shell museum, and a citrus grove in rural Arcadia. We ate lunch out regularly and agreed that we never had anything less than superb meals.

No description of that very busy January would be complete without including my birthday. Although I continued to be an early riser, I had not felt compelled to write a single note until January 24, the day after I turned 70. I described the milestone in great detail, calling it "fun, thanks to Kris, who made it a memorable day from start to finish. (Actually, I declared the birthday officially started the day before, when I played golf and we went to Bella Napoli for pizza.)"

Surprises, whimsy, serenades, cards, gifts, voicemails, Facebook wishes — all for me — made me as happy as a 7-year-old. We ended the day by splurging on my Key lime birthday pie — with its 70 flamingo picks and 7-0 candles — (overdoing our portions, truth be told). It was a fitting closing touch to the day, one I could not have enjoyed more. Nor could it have been more special.

Somehow Kris had managed to buy that pie and keep it cool and hidden away. She also had managed to get cinnamon pastries for breakfast, decorations and Amazon deliveries into the condo without my knowledge. She had decorated after I went to bed, so I woke to a flamingo tablecloth, a birthday banner with flamingos, a flamingo gift bag and flamingo cards. While she slept, I made coffee, which I drank from a flamingo party cup, and read as usual. When she got up, she sang "Happy Birthday" and couldn't wait to bring out the pie.

Before our day started in earnest, we worked out at Planet Fitness, something I could not have envisioned a couple years earlier. The forecast was for sunny and 80 degrees, so we had decided to go to Venice, eat at a beachside restaurant a friend had recommended, and explore. Which is what we did. Venice was beautiful, with a gorgeous boulevard lined with shops. Lo and behold, there was a quilt shop, which made Kris happy. She found plenty of fabric unique to the area and signed up for a class to learn to hook fabric rugs like our Granny made. What I found weird was a street full of "beachy" shops and restaurants, but mostly "old folks" where it felt as if there should be young people. I was allowed such a thought on my birthday.

When we made our way to the restaurant on Venice Beach, we once again found parking at a premium, and sure enough Sharkey's had a long wait for an outdoor table. Hungry, we opted for indoors, which turned out to be a screened porch — the perfect choice. When it came time to order, I was all set to go with the grouper special, a "safe" choice because I love that fish. But at the last second, I opted for a seafood dish with a decidedly Asian touch. This was a day to try something new. I wasn't disappointed, either in the food or in myself. Not long after, on our way out of town, I pointed to a restaurant offering "authentic Cuban food." We need to try that after your class, I told Kris. Another first.

It had been too windy for the beach, so we were heading back to Punta Gorda earlier than expected. Kris said it was a shame to end our adventure, and I was tasked with suggesting something because, after all, it was my birthday. I remembered seeing a sign for the Boca Grande historic lighthouse, and that is the turn we made. The drive to Gasparilla Island was pleasant, with gorgeous homes galore. At the lighthouse museum, I bought a coffee mug that I used every morning for the rest of our stay. We agreed that although we enjoyed visiting, we probably would be banned from living on the island because we favored T-shirts over Lily Pulitzer.

I did not write another morning note until almost a month after my birthday. I was content. I did write a postcard to ME every week, but refrained from checking in too often with the nursing home. It felt awkward at first, but I got beyond that, and when I *needed* to hear what I knew — she was doing well — I called. Mike and Caryl had promised to visit her regularly, which they did. They always texted me a photo. "She looked good," they wrote after their first visit. That was all I needed to know. My heart smiled every time I used my phone because my lock-screen image was her photo from our pre-Christmas afternoon together. She is looking directly at me, a slight smile, her hands folded together. I think she looks regal, beautiful. I think she was present in the moment, which is why I was comfortable using the photo. It was important to see her as she is, not as she was.

What a gift, to have that image. Because of it, ME's was the first face I saw each morning because I could not help immediately checking to make sure there had been no overnight messages. I had missed one a few weeks earlier, a call with news of another seizure. That was jolting — and for the first hours unnerving. But blood tests were fine, and when Mike visited a couple days later he found her "the best since Christmas." I started to think that perhaps the seizures served to "clear the cobwebs" for her.

For me, as I wrote, I realized that "our days [in Florida] have some of the same rhythms of my days at home, and there is nothing wrong with that. But conversation and exploring and doing things has been a wonderful treat. Sometimes a couple hours, sometimes most of a day." One Sunday we ventured north a couple hours, to Tarpon Spring (sponge capital of the world). From there, we were off to Tampa and lunch with ME's oldest grand-niece, a freshman at the University of Tampa. Other days, the farthest we went was Planet Fitness. If we were restless and without a plan, I was fond of finding a town on the map and researching what we might do there. That is how we found Solomon's Castle in tiny Ona. As soon as I read that its exterior was covered in discarded aluminum printing plates, I knew we had to see it. We were not disappointed.

Of all the ways we spent our time, I surprised myself most when I decided to try my hand at something "crafty." Kris makes beautiful quilts, and had been able to bring her sewing machine and a giant container of fabric, which she added to when we stopped at every specialty store we found. I had not sewn since 4-H and had no interest in re-learning. But I had brought with me a loop-yarn project I was hopeful Kris could explain. (I had failed miserably at starting it on my own.) It took some doing, but I finally made a small lap-blanket. Then another. Next thing I knew, I had bought several more kits — and kits to make fleece tie blankets. What was I thinking? I was thinking how I could give them to the nursing home for residents.

I might have been 1,400 miles away, but I knew that it was my trust in the SKNRC staff and administrators that made my winter possible. I told them as much in the handwritten Christmas letters I had written to them. I made it a point to thank them whenever I called, and instead of souvenirs for myself, I bought Florida "treats" for the big Valentine's box I sent them.

As I looked forward to our last month in Florida, I wrote: "How great it is to greet the morning with the door to the lanai open. Cool, fresh air. Watching egrets across the lake, their white moving slowly along the bank. Bird sounds as the sun rises make my heart smile. . . . I am grateful for what I have, for the gift of these last two months and the one to come."

By then, I had committed to a bigger, more expensive condo for winter 2020. Not buying John's condo had been "the absolute right decision," although I still found myself sometimes "wishing it were otherwise. . . . Good thing I generally have powerful self-control and a reasonable me usually prevails. I keep reminding myself of the years of winters I can have for the money it would cost to own. . . . *I commit to those adventures* and will work to not ruminate over the thousands of dollars already paid for next winter."

Month three flew by. Kris and I continued to fill our days; more than one friend expressed amazement at how much we did and saw. When we planned a trip to Key West after Fred's return, we somehow overlooked that it would be the height of Spring Break season. We all found too many people and too much traffic. Kris and I did spend a couple hours walking Duvall Street. It was 85 degrees, and by the time we got to the southernmost point marker, we were worn out. We skipped the picture-taking line and photobombed the tourists at its head with our selfie. A lovely coral beach on our drive back to Key Largo suited us more, as did seeing alligators from a boardwalk at a Big Cypress National Preserve visitors center. Key West was the trip I had wanted to celebrate my birthday, so I was happy we pulled it off. I only wish I had read Lucy Burdette's Key West Food Critic series *before* we planned our trip. Next time . . . .

When Kris, ME and I vacationed on Fort Myers Beach in January 2012, the new spring training facility for the Red Sox was under construction. Now Kris and I were eager to be able to attend a game there. We had just begun the 45-minute drive south when I got a text from Caryl saying ME's younger brother was dying. What a shock. That none of us knew, that Mike found out in a roundabout way, was even more shocking. Three days later, Ed was dead. It had been only a month ago that his Valentine's Day card to ME was forwarded to Florida. In a text, I reminded him that he could send mail directly to her and a staff member would read it to her. (It was a family joke that all his cards ended the same way: Hope to see you soon. At most he visited her three times after she left home.)

My heart broke for Mike, who had lost his second brother and was losing his sister. The brief wake was for immediate family only; the funeral was by invitation. I was never called. I never once considered returning home early. ME would have been devastated by the news and aghast at the secrecy. As her cousin Jane wrote me, "She could still talk about [her older brother's] death as if it were yesterday." We agreed to not tell her about Ed. It almost certainly would not mean anything and, if by chance it did, it would just cause her profound sadness. To this day, however, I have not forgiven her sister-in-law for behaving as if ME did not exist, as if we all were outsiders.

In the midst of that drama, Kris, Fred and I prepared for our leave-taking. A week before my flight, thanks to a rainy day that kept us inside, I packed several boxes for shipping. I played two final rounds of golf before packing my clubs. "I am taking out a bank loan to pay for shipping stuff home," I joked in an email to my friend Sandra. I also tried to get as much pool time as possible. I anticipated that re-entry would be difficult, not least because the forecast *highs* for Rhode Island were cooler than our *lows*. "But it is spring, and I will try to be patient and accept what is," I wrote to myself. I did ask Sandra to visit my house before I arrived and set the thermostats to 70. "I am prepared for my body to rebel," I explained. "We have had the AC set at 76 since we arrived. I imagine a cold is in my future."

I wrote myself a more optimistic note about the state of mind I would return with. "I do hope that once home I will work on gardens et al regularly, as weather permits. I also hope I can carry through with fewer visits to SKNRC without guilt. One thing being here has given me is a carefree approach to the days that feels great. That is not to say I don't miss ME. . . . My wish for her safety and health, peace and some joy, and declaration of love still end my greeting to the world each morning. And I often awake thinking of her or some period in our life. *But I can [now] go through a day doing my thing and not have her in my consciousness.*"

On our last day in Punta Gorda, I was up first as usual. As I watched dawn arrive, a poem spilled out onto my iPad:

I must fix this view in my mind's eye

The coming of dawn over Lake Rio

My soul feeling the promise

Of another day in paradise

That has been this winter

So that when the gloomy, gray, rainy, cold days

Of April in Rhode Island —

To which I am returning,

And which I anticipate with dread —

Greet me and fill the day

I can remember how many peaceful dawns I greeted

And find contentment in memory

That allows me to be happy with what is

And not sad about missing what was

Or thinking too much about what might be

Or what surely will be.

". . . Feelings came at me so hard and so fast I needed to remember that the goal was not getting rid of the feelings, but letting them flow through me."

The Bookshop at Water's End
Patti Callahan Henry

CHAPTER 11

Confronting a Crisis

We had eaten our first Punta Gorda meal at Peace River Seafood and agreed that is where we wanted to go for our last lunch. We all chose to have our last taste be Key lime pie. On the drive back to the condo, we pledged this would be our tradition. I found comfort in knowing that even though part of me was not ready to leave, I could look forward to returning.

The next morning we were on the road to Tampa International Airport at 7 o'clock. I had slept fitfully, my usual pre-travel anxieties compounded by anticipating bittersweet goodbyes and uncertain hellos. After curbside hugs, I breezed through check-in and security (thank you TSA PreCheck) and found my gate. Because I had three hours until my flight, I chose a sit-down restaurant and enjoyed a leisurely breakfast and my book. I also made it a point to do a purposeful walk of at least a mile, determined to not lose my Planet Fitness momentum. After an uneventful flight to Baltimore, I had another long layover, with more reading and more walking, followed by the short flight to Hartford. I had left my car with Mike and Caryl; it was nice to be met by family, not a shuttle driver. It was nice to return to conversation and not silence.

Mike often jokes about my punctuality. I always have taken pride in being on time. I awoke very early that Sunday, but remained in bed until 6, then made myself at home downstairs for coffee and reading. I wanted to leave by 9:30 in order to get to the nursing home before lunch. I did. Later, I wrote about arriving this way: "I didn't know what to expect . . . so I just took a deep breath and headed in. The selfie I took a couple minutes into my homecoming was visible proof that it was the best I had hoped for. ME was very good, responded to me like it was December, rolled her eyes at something I said, and surprised me after I did my Arnold Schwarzenegger impression of 'I'll be back' by parroting it back to me."

Those 25 minutes with ME energized me. I had not planned on unpacking much, but ended up unpacking everything. I made the master bathroom *mine* by replacing our flowered shower curtain with a flamingo one and adding a bath mat with palm trees. Next year I need to get towels, I said to myself. I had flamingo sheets waiting to be laundered, new flamingo kitchen towels, a spoon holder from the Peace River Wildlife Center (decorated with manatees) on the stove, a flamingo breakfast bowl and my coffee cup. I covered the coffee table in the den with the flamingo table runner Kris had made for my birthday, on top of which rested a display of shells I had collected. Choosing to make such changes felt like an important statement: I don't need to have the house look like it did when ME was here. I can redecorate for me without erasing her.

The day was gray and rainy; I went out only for a few groceries. My internet would not be restored until midnight, so for entertainment I read — and managed to make it to 9 p.m. I was not happy to sleep under flannel sheets and a down comforter; perhaps that is why it was a fitful night. I was not happy to find how much earlier dawn was. Later, I texted Kris how weird it was that for the first time in 3 1/2 months there was no one saying good morning to me.

The empty house and the silence overwhelmed me. So did facing the reality of all there was to do — inside and out. Wow, that did not take long. Rather than run from feeling lonely and overwhelmed, I acknowledged my feelings. And decided to "veg" and begin tackling my to-do list on Tuesday. I did visit ME before lunch. The "regulars" were working and it was great to chat with them. In late afternoon, I needed to write about the "restless energy coupled with malaise" that had enveloped me. "Perhaps I am being sucked in by a return of responsibility, of which there was little [in Florida]. Perhaps I need to figure out how to replace myself into life here. Stay tuned!"

At the end of my first week home, I still could not get warm. Annoying. Lying in bed one early morning, I began enumerating what I missed about Florida, and concluded the most significant was absence of responsibility. "Now home, I cannot seem to find a sense of how I want to be," I wrote. "Did I really need to tackle the guest room this week? Yes, I have made a bit of progress, but I also feel overwhelmed by the magnitude of preparing the house for my next step (unknown). It was easy in Florida to say I was ready to begin the downsizing process. Now I am not sure I am any closer to answering the how and where of my future than I was before Florida. But I will continue my journey of puzzling it out."

My brain was a jumble again. I once more had a lot on my plate. Topping the list: transitioning ME to Hospice. The nurse who months before had raised the notion of palliative care suggested it might be time for this next step. I was momentarily taken aback, but I respected her and I could not see a downside to doing so. It happened quickly, and remarkably easily. It soon would prove to be an especially prescient decision.

As had been the case pre-Florida, I once more was a frequent visitor to the nursing home, sometimes primarily to tend to the gardens I had planted, but always to spend time with ME. We shared the noon meal on Easter (April 21) at a small table with N, once ME's roommate, and P. My discomfort over such an arrangement was long gone, and we had a pleasant meal. ME, who required a lot of help, ate well; N and P still managed for themselves. P could be a handful, but was in a good space; an aide commented that she never had seen her sit still for an entire meal. I like to think I helped create a vibe that was comfortable for all. I was content when I left, as was ME, who was watching Mass on TV.

Although it was drizzly, I was not ready to go home. I decided to take a drive, as ME and I had been so fond of doing. I headed to Point Judith, where it was quite foggy. I got a great photo of the Coast Guard station and lighthouse. Once home, I was still restless, so I began cleaning out a small bookcase filled with ME's things — and dust bunnies. I went through a pile of cards, most from me to her, the dates all over the place. I did a quick read of most, then put them in a bag for recycling. That was not difficult. I was not sure why until it occurred to me that my actions over the last few years spoke volumes more than the words I had written. Those actions also told me that I had meant what I wrote — even when I doubted that. I reminded myself how I was doing my best to honor the love those cards professed.

Surely the seriousness with which I sorted ME's stuff honored that love. More than one friend and family member told me they would have just pitched everything. Even though it was a slog, I could see progress with each bag of recycling and trash, with each emptied shelf or drawer. Of course, there also were the "second look" piles — and the give to so-and-so piles. But wouldn't it be fun when I could bring Mike the first dollar from their dad's store?!

All that sorting — I committed to an hour a day but usually did more — left my brain awash in memories. Time and again I recalled when choosing a card had been difficult because I had mixed feelings and could not bring myself to give ME a card that expressed a sentiment I really wasn't feeling. I wrote about that: "The rough spots along the way. I wonder at times how we made it through them . . . neither of us strong in the communication department, especially me. Especially at times of conflict." I also had found "a couple of pieces of writing that showed a depth of pain within ME that I didn't comprehend. Or I had forgotten. [But which] clearly haunted her forever."

My reaction to those writings led me to think about regrets, after I acknowledged to myself that contrary to what I have said often, I *do* have them. I realized the brain goes where it wants to go, I told my therapist, and these days I was less inclined to try to control that. I described the two regrets that had been haunting me. The first was losing my temper when we got home late from a trip. It was hot, the house was unbearable, and I asked ME to go upstairs, open the windows and turn on the fans. When I finally got up there, she had done nothing and was fiddling with something. "Can't you do anything?!" I remember screaming. What I know looking backward in time is that she likely was confused by my instructions. The disease was there; we just didn't know it.

My second regret, I told Beverly, was that ME and I never talked about her dementia, never took advantage of the time after her MCI diagnosis to plan. I thought I was being respectful of her need for privacy and right to make decisions. Really, though, I was scared and I didn't know how to respond when she *would* say something like, "When I get better. . . ."

A few days later, I added a third regret to my list: "I wasn't emotionally available to you for months and months and months," I wrote. That one bubbled up after I heard the journalist Katie Couric say that when her husband was in his nine-month battle with colon cancer, she was so afraid of him thinking she had given up hope that they never had a conversation about the possibility of him dying. And, she said, she remains haunted by that. "Ah . . . I am not alone," I thought. It wasn't long before I would be haunted by a seemingly benign gesture I connected to a health crisis that had us believing ME was dying.

It started with a small stuffed chick I had brought to ME in early May. She was always fiddling with things and I thought it would give her something to occupy her hands. It seemed to disappear by the next day and I thought nothing more about it — until the nurse called to say she saw ME trying to eat it. Turns out the feet had tiny beads of some sort, and it was unclear if ME had swallowed any. But she had vomited a couple of times, was very tired and uninterested in eating. The next day the nurse called to say ME was more alert, but was experiencing abdominal pain. The Hospice nurse checked on her mid-afternoon and said she clearly was in distress, the source unclear. I raised the issue of the beads, which she was aware of. It could be related to that, she allowed, but not necessarily. I supported doing an X-ray in hopes of identifying the cause. But then what,

I wondered as my mind raced ahead. Would this be the incident that resulted in me saying "no further treatment, just do what is necessary to keep her comfortable"? I tried to channel my therapist — without much luck — in order to stay in the moment.

For me, there is only one way to describe that day and those that followed: the roller coaster was off and running again, ME's dementia in control. I was not prepared for the ride. I was not prepared for the waiting, the uncertainties. I kept Mike and Caryl informed from the start, but didn't want to share the possible outcomes until I knew more. When the first X-ray was inconclusive, another was ordered. When I talked with the Hospice nurse late the next afternoon, she was still waiting on results. We reviewed the options in the event that the suspected bowel blockage was confirmed: (1) more workups, meaning more tests because the goal would be to treat, thus requiring leaving Hospice; (2) keep ME comfortable — *until death* went unspoken.

I finally talked with Mike the next morning. Even though I was empowered to make the decision, I would not do so without him and Caryl. Thankfully, we were on the same page: The second option was the one best for ME; what would be the point of the other? When I hung up, I wrote later, "I could say that I am at peace with the decision, if that is what it comes to. And surely, if it turns out not to be now, it will be at some point down the road. Nonetheless, it is gut-wrenching. Impossible not to think of what the days ahead might be like. To anticipate my hurt, my sorrow. I need to allow myself to feel whatever. And to take the day one step at a time. *That is how I can honor ME, our love, our life, myself.*"

The news from the Hospice nurse when I called the following morning was, as she put it, "not great," although it was less dire than I expected.

The second X-ray showed no bowel obstruction but there was a "moderate ileus." Something was preventing her bowel from working correctly. The plan was to ensure ME's comfort and restrict her to liquids for a couple of days. The nurse would assess the situation on Friday (May 10). "Wait, watch, hope" were the words I wrote in my notes. I could feel a physical release of tension as I absorbed the news, and at least in the moment the immediate future felt different than I had been imagining. I tried to convey that when I talked with Mike a bit later. When I visited ME about 2, she was sleeping so soundly she did not even stir when I bent down to kiss her and say I love you. Her aide said she had been very sleepy all day, but she had gotten her to drink.

My day(s) felt surreal. I understand that pregnant women often "nest" when labor is near, and I wondered if my second round of photo sorting/timeline making was a similar sort of response. That somewhere deep in my psyche (or perhaps not so deep) I had begun to prepare for ME's death. How else to explain beginning to plan her funeral? Searching Joan Chittister's book *The Gift of Years/Growing Old Gracefully* for something I might use and reading a spot-on essay about memories. Making a list of items I might put in her casket. Wondering about music, readings, speakers. "I don't choose to go there," I wrote in a note, "but I am pulled there by forces outside my understanding."

At the same time, I had to make decisions about me. Should I go to Connecticut on Saturday for ME's goddaughter's First Communion? Should I go to the ballet on Sunday? Should I leave for three nights in Maine on Tuesday? I held off telling friends what was happening until I knew more. I did bring Mike and Caryl up to date with a long text, and made clear they were welcome to come over for the Hospice nurse's visit.

"She thinks the increasing lethargy is not from meds alone. Is concerned that we will see a steady decline going forward." I noted that ME had been moved off the liquid diet, which I found comforting, but said I planned to cancel Maine "unless there is a startling difference tomorrow." I ended with the news that "the move is likely happening Monday."

Oh yes, the move. In the midst of our crisis, the social worker called to tell me that ME was being moved from PondView to a room in the nursing home's main section. Because she was not a wanderer, and because there was an increased need for beds in the locked unit, they deemed the move appropriate. The social worker assured me they had a good roommate match in a nice room with a window bed. I was thrown for a loop. Eventually, however, I realized the move and its timing felt awful for me, because of my comfort level with PondView staff and residents, but made sense for ME. Trust the professionals, I told myself.

After I saw the room and met the nurse and a CNA, I decided that it would be OK. Then I went home, got into comfy clothes, finished sorting photos from 2002, and drafted an obituary. That had been on my mind. Who better to do it, after all? It was short and sweet. I didn't want a cookie-cutter job and didn't want a tome that screamed, "Look how important I was." Finally, I started a list of who we would need to contact. In my mind, it made sense to do those things while I "sort of have my wits about me," I noted.

Visits with ME after my return from Florida had been unpredictable. Sometimes she was alert, sometimes not. Sometimes she was sleepy; sometimes she was asleep. There was no way of knowing whether I would stay a few minutes or an hour. I quickly learned to be OK with the ME I found. Wishing she were otherwise would not make her so. Holding her hand for a few minutes as she dozed could be enough. And when she offered more — such as on April 27 — my heart would smile for days. That day, as I always did before leaving, I had kissed her and said, "I love you." That day she responded, "I love you too." What a wonderful gift!

With her health crisis, the dread I felt walking into the nursing home during her first weeks there returned. Never more so than the Friday I was to meet with the Hospice nurse. I awoke filled with nervous energy and could not seem to get warm, my personal stress meter sending me strong signals. It had been a miserable night. I dozed in the recliner, but when I went to bed and turned on HGTV, even that did not lull me to sleep. I finally turned it off, only to toss and turn and ruminate for what felt like forever. I tried the TV again after midnight, but had a difficult time finding something mindless. More dozing; TV off again. Sleep came sometime after 2 but stayed only until 5. I didn't remain in bed long. When I greeted the world, my thanks were general. I was on the verge of breaking down. The overcast dawn fit my mood; my stomach was in knots. I read in a mental fog. "I so wish I could stop the dread," I noted.

Instead, I carried it with me into the nursing home, where I was pleasantly surprised to find ME in her wheelchair and alert. It was lunchtime, and because the Hospice nurse was coming I wheeled her to the back room for a table and quiet. We were able to visit a bit and I helped her start on a glass of juice. A Hospice aide actually arrived first; she had been there the day before, to help ME with her lunch, and so I let her do that when the time came. When the nurse arrived, we chatted as she assessed ME. All her vitals were within reason. Then a Hospice social worker arrived, and I joked we might as well have a party.

Actually, we had more than an hour visiting with ME and talking. ME was sleepy, but they wanted to give her time to digest lunch before she went for a nap. Later, I wrote that I was "thankful to have had this time with her; it was good to have her awake and present." I also warned myself, "I must beware of the roller coaster, I know." Although they did not make it in time for the meeting, Mike and Caryl visited ME later that afternoon. I left our First Communion gifts for them.

Saturday was not an easy day, but by the evening I was "eerily calm." Perhaps the result of facing fears and doing difficult things. I had correctly chosen not to go to Connecticut for the First Communion; I was physically and emotionally exhausted. I made that decision knowing the gold cross Lexy longed for would be there, a loving gift from her godmother. And early that morning, when I texted my friend Linda to say I was not up to the ballet, I knew that was taking care of me, as everyone on Friday urged me to do. So was admitting I was not comfortable being three hours away for three nights, and canceling my Maine trip.

Nervous energy again propelled me to late morning, when I went to the nursing home thinking I could help ME with lunch. She was in the main room, sound asleep and snoring in her new wheelchair. She did not stir, so I got her fleece "ice cream" blanket, handmade by my sister, covered her and sat with her. The nurse said she had not eaten or drunk anything that morning, which I found worrisome. After I kissed her and said goodbye, I told the nurse (who was doing a double shift) I would probably be back.

I was trying to eat mindfully, but was not interested in making meals, so I went to McDonald's for a WW-friendly salad. Once home, it was time for another difficult duty: telephone calls. I called ME's longtime friend

Joan, hoping to leave a message but she answered. Drat. The conversation went about as I expected. At one point she asked if I thought ME was "fighting," which I heard as "fighting not to die." I said I would not put it that way; rather she was transitioning and responding in the ways we do at the end stage of life. (The pamphlet I had kept from when my father was dying and a similar one the Hospice nurse gave me proved their value.) Later she asked if she should come. I had the good sense to tell her I could not answer that, then explained how she likely would find ME if she were to come.

Next up was ME's cousin Jane, also a difficult call, but in a different way. Jane is the cousin ME was closest to. And Jane has been a rock for me since the beginning of this journey. She was caring and wise, appreciative of me and supportive. Ours was a good talk, after the initial shock of the news. There were tears, but also some laughter. Assurances that I was doing the right things. And, as always, a reminder that I must also think about myself.

I returned to the nursing home in late afternoon and was pleasantly surprised to find ME with her eyes open. The nurse and aides said the same thing. I asked them for a glass of juice and said I would try to get her to drink. Success. She seemed to forget how to swallow and sometimes wanted to bite the glass. From somewhere I found enormous patience, realized she sometimes responded to prompts, and so we took it one sip at a time. I was not optimistic when her meal arrived, but over time I got her to eat several bites of vegetable, a couple bites of potato and of meat — all pureed. And the entire ice cream cup (no surprise there!). Finally, she managed most of a nutritional drink. I did not force anything, let her refuse, then would try again. I knew that eating or not was up to her. I knew enough to allow that.

What amazed me almost as much as my patience were the several sentences I found in my notes describing ME's tablemates that evening. The passage reminds me how I had come to "know" them as individuals, was attuned to their personalities, behaviors and quirks. How I could talk with them, accepting them in a way I could not have envisioned months before. For example, that night J was sitting next to me. She was a former roommate of ME's, and was by then blind. As she carried on a conversation with an imaginary dog, I joined in. I elicited quite a chuckle when I said his name was Buster, as in Buster Brown shoes.

After 6, with ME beginning to nod off, I told her I needed to go and have my own supper. As always, I hugged her, gave her a kiss, and said "See you later, alligator." Then I did it all again before I headed to the door, being sure to thank the staff on my way out. In my car, I checked my phone for messages (a behavior I thought I was unlikely to lose any time soon), took a deep breath and said aloud to the World, "Thanks for this time." During the drive home, I talked to myself about how feeding ME was an expression of love, its own kind of intimacy, and how I was grateful for such moments.

Sunday was a gray, rainy Mother's Day. In my den, a lone tulip from those I had picked on my visit to Wicked Tulips flower farm remained, its red and yellow beauty straight and tall in a Waterford vase. When I first saw it that morning, I wrote, "I thought of ME, her quiet beauty and dignity still visible to me, if only momentarily, during this transition."

I was expecting Connecticut family members to visit, and had told them it was possible ME would not be awake. It was important to me that they know what to expect. I also sent a text to ME's niece in Massachusetts to let her know that "ME's health has failed considerably over the last couple weeks and she is in the end stage of Alzheimer's. No way of predicting the length of that, of course, but didn't want you surprised when the end does come. Please share with your mother and [sister]." As for me, I was working at taking it one step at a time.

Although ME's status still felt dire, that Sunday provided a bit of relief for us all. When I arrived, I was told she had eaten a good breakfast, and she ate a good lunch for me. When the Connecticut gang arrived, ME was engaged and clearly enjoyed the time with her nieces, nephew and grand-niece. She showed no signs of discomfort, and when a Hospice nurse stopped in she found her vitals to be good. Perhaps the best evidence of my mood was the fact that even though I had time to write Sunday evening, I made a conscious decision not to. I gave myself a break from the crisis, and when I did write the next morning I didn't attempt my customary blow-by-blow record. The calm before another storm.

ME's move from PondView was almost as big a gut punch for me as confronting the reality of end-stage Alzheimer's. Going to the nursing home late Monday morning to find her in her chair, parked out in the new space. Walking to her old room and seeing the bed made and a Welcome note on it. Going to her new room and finding her clothes stuffed in bags, other belongings piled on the chair and bed. And staff I didn't know, except by sight.

When I returned at supper time, the nurse and aides (again "strangers") were flat-out busy. Then and there I decided I would stay to feed her. I noticed ME looked uncomfortably positioned in her wheelchair, and I did manage to get a pillow for her. I was happy when her tray was among the first delivered, and happy that she ate and drank fairly well. Nonetheless, it was difficult to leave her.

I was a mess. I slept little. Mind aswirl, a physical aching. I needed to *do* something, but what? I could see that the last six-plus years had been a series of "small" losses, and this move was another. After a couple hours of ruminating, it became clear that I needed a face-to-face with the social worker. I called and left that message. I sorted photos, increasingly impatient and frustrated as time passed and I did not get a call. I knew that was unreasonable, but in the moment I needed to be priority No. 1. Then, just as I was about to call again, my phone rang. Meeting set for late afternoon with social worker and admissions director.

I rehearsed all sorts of scenarios. I don't do rage, but I was working on it. Luckily, in the couple of hours I had to kill before the meeting, I found my equilibrium and my strategy: I would simply ask if there were any possibility of returning ME to PondView. That is all I really wanted/needed to know. The answer would guide the discussion to follow. So that is what I asked. The decision, I was told, could be reviewed but not before a 30-day tryout. More important, as we talked I was able to acknowledge that my distress over the move was probably more about me than ME. I made it clear that I was confident her good care would continue, but also described the things bothering me: how I found her belongings, how I was concerned that she would not get the attention she was used to, how I feared she would not get the time she needed when eating.

They reminded me that the staff would need time to get to know ME, which had been true in PondView, too. Ditto for me getting to know them. I assured them that I really did believe they were looking out for ME — and me. I also told them that I would continue to advocate for ME and would not be shy about saying when I thought something was amiss. I left the office optimistic that all would feel fine in 30 days.

ME was sleeping, so I sat with her and gently, slowly got her to wake up. The activities director stopped to say hi and tell me that ME had enjoyed the music Monday afternoon. That was reassuring. ME responded to her, but nothing like the way her face lit up when the environmental services director said hello. ME gave her a smile as wide as I had seen in a very long time. Both of those interactions reminded me that there were lots of eyes and hearts keeping watch over her. Dinner was early because of a family party that evening (I had decided not to stay for that because I was too spent physically and emotionally), so I hung around to help ME. I was "rewarded" with an "I love you, too" when I took my leave.

I dropped in Wednesday afternoon to hear "Elvis," but ME was in bed and sleeping, so I did not stay. I did ask the nurse how ME was doing and got a great report: ate a good breakfast and lunch, was sleeping well, had adjusted to her new surroundings. I also popped into PondView to say hello. Later that afternoon, the Hospice nurse called, and afterward I sent a number of people this text: "[The nurse] said she had a 'good visit' with ME, pleased with vitals et al. . . . No discomfort. Said everything she observed is 'baseline ME,' and I don't think she was expecting that. Knock wood. One day at a time. But a heck of a lot better than a week ago!"

It seemed to me that ME's situation had stabilized, that the crisis was over. Our latest roller coaster ride — a week long — had slowed. A few days later, I wrote about visiting ME late on Saturday morning and finding her asleep. About that same time on Sunday, she again was sleeping — soundly. I moved her arms effortlessly and her hands were not clenched. (The day before she had held tight to my fingers, my hand, my arm; her strength still there.) I was able to clean and file her nails with ease. I didn't stay long after that, but did chat with the nurse. After I drove away I realized I had not kissed ME or said goodbye. I drove a tad farther, did not like how I was feeling, so turned around and went back. That was the moment I committed to never leaving her without a "proper" goodbye. The rest of my day was "foggy" as I worked at processing the "now" and not getting caught up in looking too far ahead. I tried out a new mantra: *Allow the day to unfold and accept it with grace.*

Just before ME's birthday, I took note of a line I had read in a *New York Times* story about a woman with stage 4 lung cancer climbing a mountain. She was quoted as saying, "It's definitely hard being sick and saying goodbye to the person you were before." As far as I knew, ME never was able to say that goodbye because she never acknowledged her diagnosis. I, on the other hand, lately had been saying goodbye to the person she was before the latest turn in her awful ordeal. I had not thought about it that way before, but in that moment I saw it was what I did in order to accept the ME I found each day I visited. That understanding was a gift.

May 30th, on her 78th birthday, ME gave us a gift — a good couple hours while Mike, Caryl and two of their daughters visited. Numerous staff members stopped by to offer wishes, and Activities tied balloons to her wheelchair. I was able to put together a bouquet, mostly from home and including irises (her favorites) that had begun blooming just in time. Later, I thought that if this should prove to be her last birthday, I would always be grateful that it had been as good as could be. I really do think she liked being the center of attention, although the next day it was clear the celebration had exhausted her. She did not stir when I said hello, sat with her for a bit, or when I kissed her goodbye.

A day later it was clear that ME's health scare had taken a lot more out of me than I realized. I woke up with a full-blown cold, my first illness in a long time. I had no choice but to lay low — and hope that I had not infected ME (I had not). I was so miserable, I told a friend later, that if someone had shot me that weekend I would not have cared. My cold lingered more than a week with annoying congestion, and was a painful reminder of the toll stress exacts. My energy returned slowly, and even when I was restless I had to admit I had limited capacity for garden work. Long gone were my six- or eight-hour stretches of manual labor. What I now saw was an endless list of tasks, and as I undertook one another would pop up. I both wanted to accomplish something and had less and less interest in doing the work. I felt overwhelmed and discouraged. One of these days, I told myself, I need to commit to shedding this big house and yard. How will I know when? I wondered.

On a day typical of my malaise, I struggled with wanting/not wanting to go to the nursing home. Struggled with wanting/not wanting to go out for lunch. Decided on pizza, then at the last minute remembered a Mexican spot I wanted to try. What a disappointment. Afterward, I parked at the sea wall to continue reading. Even that did not satisfy. My porch was a bit better — until I felt the need to be doing. I went to the basement and one of ME's filing cabinets in search of papers to sort. My restless energy means something, I thought, but I was not sure what.

The Big Basement Cleanout, as I came to call it, was one way I channeled that energy. Another was a calendar unusually filled with activities. There were regular coffee and creative conversations with Sandra, so different in content from those before ME left home. There was another road trip to Stockbridge, Massachusetts, with my friend Linda. There was my solo visit to Sunflowers for Wishes in Griswold, Connecticut: one bouquet for me, one for ME and one for the nursing home. There were chamber music concerts with Roberta and Sandra. There was an overnight to Connecticut for pool time with family. There was gardening at home and at the nursing home.

When I was successful in allowing a day to unfold, there was a weekend such as the one I described in a Sunday evening note:

> I believe I did a good job this weekend of allowing the day(s) to unfold. [Saturday], by noon, I had cleaned, Swiffered floors, planted patio boxes and the leftover annuals. I had thought I might visit ME, but decided to keep the day for me. I enjoyed lunch on the porch, then read a bit and plotted how to enjoy the decent weather and keep from planting myself in front of TV golf. Decided to drive to Westerly for a walk and reading in Wilcox Park, and maybe DQ. Which is exactly what I did. Once home, the late afternoon and evening were much as usual.

> Today [Sunday] I slept in a bit — to about 5:30. Finished *Fly Girls*. Made my first Wonderslim pancakes. Laundered towels. Watched most of "CBS Sunday Morning" before showering. Decided to get a salad for supper before heading off to see ME. I was lucky — she was awake and alert when I arrived about 11:45. I ended up staying until 1:15 or so, and it was nice. "Mrs. Doubtfire" was playing on the TV. I was content to help ME drink her juice, then eventually feed her lunch. Had not been sure I would stay for that, but it was so nice to have her with me that I wanted to stay. On the way out, I allowed myself a couple sweets from the Father's Day treats! Grateful for the good visit. The good day.

The following Sunday was even better. I wrote:

I can't seem to find the words to describe the joy of today.

Cloudless sky, warm. Leisurely start to the day. Allowing the day to unfold until I head to the nursing home about 11. Hoping ME is awake enough to go outdoors — for first time since last fall. And she is. So I put on her hat and out we go; this big wheelchair awkward to steer. I sure don't want to pitch her out! She is "chatty." We circle the parking lot, stopping in the shade for a selfie. . . . We don't stay out too long, but I said we will do it again tomorrow if weather allows. Back inside I file her nails, which were clipped a week ago but are ragged. I decide to stay to help her with lunch. She remains alert and chatty. Ate all her breakfast, I am told, so no concern that she eats only a bit of lunch. Drinks 1 1/2 glasses of juice, though (and had three at breakfast!). I felt so content when I left, so happy for the time we had and for the fact of her having a good day.

I was content at home, too. The night before, I made it a point to go to a gallery opening because our friend Roberta was one of the artists involved. ME always ensured that we went to those, even when I was reluctant, so it felt as if I were representing us both. Although no one asked about her, I felt ME's presence and that was enough.

Monday was another good day, and in the evening I took time to write a short note about two things from the morning. I went to the nursing home early, to do some weeding before it got too hot. ME was having breakfast, and "I swear she smiled when she saw me, a twinkle in her eyes." A couple hours later, after I finished, I was taking stuff to my car but had stopped to talk with two housekeeping staff members. I did not see ME in her usual spot. Turned out she was in the room across the hall, and the Activities staffer told me that ME looked up when she heard my voice! After I washed up, I sat with her for a while. She was alert and "chatty." My heart smiled.

My night was horrible, however. My sleeplessness was primarily because of pain from the shingles vaccine I got that afternoon. I also think, however, that my body was remembering what I had not: ME had been gone from our home for two years. But, I wrote that morning, "She is more present in my heart than she had been in years. Weird, huh?"

As much as my long hello was coexisting with her long goodbye, however, I also acknowledged "moments of wondering if her disease would have progressed as it has if I had resettled her sooner, had not stayed away for several days after the move, had handled things with more kindness, less yelling. If we had been able to talk about it." Writing that — another way of owning my feelings of inadequacy — brought me back to the truth: "I don't believe any of those things would have changed the downward spiral. She is safe and well cared for. She is loved. Nothing, however, can keep her dementia at bay." As for me, I concluded, "I go forward as best I know how, learning along the way, living the life I have. That is something."

"In my acts of work and cleaning, I find solace and peace and some perspective on my thoughts."

John Connell
The Farmer's Son

CHAPTER 12

2019: Memories & More

I credit the heat and humidity that summer for my successful Big Basement Cleanout, an offshoot of the upstairs Sorting and Tossing Project. A measure of my progress in moving my life forward was my readiness to dwell in memories. Day after day of rediscovering and discovering our lives — as individuals and as a couple. The projects were both satisfying (seeing a couple square feet of floor hidden for years, for example) and aggravating (why was I stuck with doing all this alone?).

The basement was so filled with stuff, a friend remarked, that "it looks like borderline hoarding going on." Combine any two people's households and stored boxes are not unusual. Then add 25 years of their life together. And remember they are two academics, prone to collecting books and saving articles, journals, papers, course syllabi and more. Finally, recognize that one (ME), it is safe to say, did not throw out anything. It did not take me much cleaning to become convinced of that.

Just when I thought I had emptied the last box of books, I would find more. Just when I thought I was finished with university-related files, I would find more. Just when I thought I had considered the last of her memorabilia, I would unearth more cards, letters, college notebooks, convent keepsakes and more. "It really is quite incredible!" I wrote her cousin Jane. "And sometimes I just pause and read awhile. If only she were available to talk about some of this stuff." For example, there was an "aha" moment when I longed for a conversation with her about how we each came to our academic/intellectual interests in "the other." The more I sorted, the more I saw powerful ways we had "crossed paths" like this before we even knew one another.

If only I could have shared such musings with ME. Thankfully, I could allow myself to be sad about the past even as my mood would improve dramatically with the slightest hint in the present of the "real" ME. Such as after the visit when I kissed her and said "I love you" and she replied, "The same back to you." Or when I would say, "Give me a smile," and she would. Or when she would allow me to hold her hands to "reach for the sky" and stretch for a couple repetitions. Or the visit when she was sleepy and barely opened her eyes while I sat with her, but when I whispered "I love you" before I left, she whispered back, "I love you, too." As her decline continued, as she spoke less and less, I continued to harbor hope for seeing a wee bit of her. I had, however, learned the difficult but important lesson — don't expect, just accept — and that made all the difference.

I started the cleanouts thinking that I wanted to create something to reflect ME's life, but I was not at all sure what it would be. So deciding what to pass along to family or friends, what to save and what to toss, was not easy. When I found a few boxes of my things, the degree of difficulty doubled. I had watched Marie Kondo on Netflix and found the "sparks joy" approach useful with my own clothing and "trinkets," but it did not help much with ME's. So I plowed on; the amount of material I kept paled in comparison to what I recycled, repurposed or trashed. I joked to my therapist that once I finished The Big Basement Cleanout, it would be my greatest accomplishment since earning my Ph.D. That was a fitting assessment, given how many books were involved in both endeavors.

My excitement over Scrapper Guy hauling away the first load from the basement in late July was matched only by the relief I felt in August when I finally figured out what to do with more than 600 of ME's old books. Most of them had been boxed in the basement since we moved into the house in January 1991! I had hoped to avoid the landfill, and I did, but it was a challenge. Not for the first time on this dementia journey did my persistent stubbornness pay off. I got plenty of exercise as I unpacked the books in the basement, repacked them in plastic grocery bags, and carried them to the garage. Before too long, there were 52 bags of books in the garage and I had run out of bags. I found more tucked away, and a friend was happy to give me a bunch. I almost doubled the number of filled bags in the garage. After much online searching, I found an organization that would accept almost all old books. Problem was, its closest book drops were in Connecticut. Stubbornly persistent, after three two-hour roundtrips I had disposed of all the basement books.

About that same time — mid-August — I was reviewing ME's status with the Hospice nurse. We remarked on how she had not had a seizure in some time, and how she showed no ill-effects from her April crisis (her diet remained pureed, however). I wondered if that meant she might be removed from Hospice (I hoped not), and learned that if it were in the cards it would not happen immediately. When I saw ME a couple days later, I thought she was lethargic, but I got her outdoors for a few minutes anyway. The next morning, after pulling Rose of Sharon seedlings from the yard for four hours, I had a message from Mike and Caryl saying they were on their way to visit ME. I decided to skip the nursing home. They sent me a photo; ME looked good.

I was out early the next day to pull more seedlings, and when I went into the house for a break, I had a voicemail asking me to call the nurse. I figured skin tear. Wrong. Seizure! The nurse said ME was resting comfortably and Hospice had been notified. I texted the news to Mike and Caryl, and told them I would go see her. I knew from past experience that she was likely to sleep much of the day. I know it was not true, but it certainly seemed as if her brain knew when I was getting ready to travel. Such a puzzling disease.

And, I came to wonder, was that brain conspiring with the travel gods to keep me nearby? I had planned a week in northern Virginia with my nephew and family. Long story short, weather cancelled my first flight, and mid-morning the next day I pulled the plug on the rescheduled flight because the late afternoon forecast had me spooked. I did my best to let events unfold and make decisions in my best interest. I did my best to make the most of the unscheduled week I had been given.

It was during that week that I had perhaps the most satisfying result from my cleanout experiences. ME was immensely proud of her Irish heritage. She had designed and taught courses on women in Irish society, and had amassed an impressive collection of non-fiction and fiction, teaching materials, media and such. I was determined to find an appropriate home for those but — again — it was not easy. One day I was talking with her friend Fran, a nun in western Massachusetts, who offered to contact the Irish Cultural Center of Western New England, which I knew nothing about. The woman who had been helping set up their library was delighted to accept ME's collection. "This news makes my day," I wrote to her. Equally exciting, the center had once been affiliated with ME's alma mater! Days later, when I got into my car after delivering the collection, I said aloud, "ME, we just did something really, really nice." I repeated that more than once before I got home. Several weeks later, I learned that the center planned something really nice for ME: Her collection would get its own "corner" in the library!

And then, the calendar and season turned. The air felt different. The morning of September 2 (a Monday) was chilly, the grass was dew-covered. My Facebook post on Saturday had revealed my funk as I remembered how for years that had been the day when we left Hilton Head and shared many dinners in Fredericksburg, Virginia, with our friends Karen and Bev. What I didn't write, because at the time it was mostly swirling in my subconscious, was how it also marked two years since ME went to the nursing home. How far I had come since then.

I saw my therapist for the first time in three weeks on the 5th. I had talked now and again about the ideas bubbling up as I memory surfed, but based on my notes this was the first time I shared a working title for whatever project emerged: Unexpected Gifts. I told Beverly I feared what I was thinking about might be viewed as egotistical or arrogant or pretentious — characteristics I find reprehensible. She assured me I had wisdom to share. I like to think so, I said.

I marveled at how different I was from the me who had said almost apologetically, "Caregiving is not in my wheelhouse." The me who dreaded walking into the nursing home. I shared an anecdote about working in "my" gardens outside PondView and stopping in the back room to say hi to C. She was sitting alone, staring at the television. "It's so nice to see you," I said. She grinned and slowly stood. I told her I was stinky and sweaty from working outside, but she clearly wanted a hug. So I gave her one, then helped her to sit. There was a big smile on her face, her eyes were bright. She threw me a kiss; I returned it. I said goodbye and walked away feeling *good*. In that moment, I realized my heart was big enough to share.

Over the months, I had watched residents come and go from PondView, had watched individuals deteriorate (sometimes slowly and other times quickly), had learned the behaviors of many, had grown increasingly comfortable interacting with several. It took me awhile, but I was able to call every staff member by name, could ask about their health, their kids and grandkids, could tell whether it was a good or bad day on the unit. I felt at home there. It never was quite like that in ME's new unit, except with the 7-11 nurses and aides. I finally adjusted to visiting before lunch, not after, and regularly spoke to a couple of residents. I continued to enjoy interacting with staff from all the departments; I tried to never let a visit go by without thanking someone.

My "allow the day to unfold" mantra had made a real difference in my life, and it continued into the fall. Although I love the season's crisp air, I hate the disappearing daylight as the days grow shorter. On September 25, a weatherman said we would not have as much daylight again until mid-March. My body seemed to know that; my mind was all over the place, jumping ahead and ahead. I tried to let each day unfold, but often needed to remind myself repeatedly. How was it that the day before I *was* able to live in the moment? To make a last-minute decision to not play golf, but to go for a walk on Narragansett beach. I couldn't remember the last time I had walked *on* the beach; how nice it felt to be there again. I did think a bit about all the beach walks with ME, and for a while I missed having her by my side. Yet I also marveled at how lucky I am to live just 15 minutes away. And how I was not ready to leave this — or my house — just yet. Back home, I continued to go with the flow. Read on the porch. Ate lunch on the porch. Took my list of woodchuck-averse plants to a nearby nursery having a buy one/get one sale and bought six pots for the nursing home. Finished organizing my items for the nursing home yard sale.

Reviewing my notes, I see how the fall was a period of transition for me. Since ME's health crisis, shortly after I returned from Florida, I probably had spent more time at SKNRC than when she first was admitted. I had not planned to do so, and ME didn't know if I had been there a day ago or a week ago. But I knew. I visited frequently because I *wanted* to, not because I felt obligated to. Now, however, it was time to pull back — so I could handle absence. October began two months of travel, and then I would be off to Florida after Christmas.

I enjoyed three nights in Maine; five days later I left for Wisconsin for our Sisters Weekend — grown to nine days. After being home for a few days, I was off to Virginia for my "makeup" week (no weather cancelation this time). Home again, for less than a week, I flew to Hilton Head for a week with Libby and John. It was the first time I flew directly to the island, and I couldn't help but remember the second trip ME and I made there.

The only choice then was Savannah, but in between our first trip and our next, they opened a new terminal. We didn't know. "I don't remember taxiing this long," I commented to ME after we landed. "I hope we are in Savannah."

On one of those October days when I wasn't away, I found myself cleaning out our "travel rack" in the study, where we stashed all sorts of materials from trips taken and trips wished for. I had not set out to clean, but my computer was updating software and one thing led to another. Next thing I knew I was remembering trips and sightseeing and realizing again how much we had done pre-dementia. I made extensive notes about each finding; some day that timetable will come in handy, I thought. Coincidentally, one of my Facebook memories that day was from a Sisters Weekend that started with an overnight near Kenosha, Wisconsin. While hanging out in our hotel room after dinner, I asked Kris, "Do you think when we are old we will still wear hoodies and jeans?" She was certain we would. And we still do.

Other than ME having two seizures (a first) the day I arrived in Wisconsin, and chilly, wet Hilton Head weather that meant no golf, my trips were spectacular. I landed in Washington early the morning after the Nationals won the World Series and got the T-shirt I hoped for. "Nothing better than glee and hugs at preschool and bus stop," I wrote of my Virginia grandnephews. What a stretch of love from family and friends.

Still, settling in after four trips in five weeks proved a challenge, and I often found myself feeling at loose ends. There were the occasional reminders of how it was six years since ME had received the MCI diagnosis. Much as I resisted, I once more found myself wondering how "today" would be if we had handled things differently. Or did the years play out as they had because we are who we are, and we stayed true to form? "But it does not matter, does it?" I wrote. "Today would be today for ME. The disease rules her life — came to rule her life. There would be no changing that. What could change — and has changed — is me. I continue to be a work in progress, and hope to be until I leave the world. For that I am grateful." Ironically, I had not written this kind of reflection — once an almost daily undertaking — in some time. Now the need bubbled up and I responded.

Another reason for feeling at loose ends was that I had begun to plan for Florida even as I decompressed from my recent travels. My second winter away would be different because I would drive — alone to Virginia, then with my sister to Punta Gorda. I already was making lists of tasks to button up the house, deadlines for all sorts of actions, what to pack, etc. I would be alone for a couple of two-week stretches, and I was determined to use them as my "writer's retreat." That required me to gather enough materials to get started on the book that remained little more than an amorphous idea.

Being away for the holidays felt right my first year alone. This year, and especially given April's scare, it felt right to spend those days with ME. If these should be her last Thanksgiving and Christmas, I wanted to have shared them with her.

She was dozing when I arrived about 11:30 Thanksgiving morning, so I popped into PondView to greet staff and residents. I made a point of saying "thanks for all you do" to each staff member. I returned to a still drowsy ME, so I held her hand and chatted with a woman whose mother's wheelchair usually was next to ME. (Only in Rhode Island: The woman had been an aide for ME in memory care.) Eventually ME perked up, in time for a traditional (albeit pureed) turkey dinner. She ate so-so, par for the course at lunch. I enjoyed every bite of my meal, including the pumpkin pie. When ME ate only a few bites of filling from hers, I kept the rest for my Friday breakfast — and then scored a slice untouched by a resident. The only leftover that really mattered to me was pie, and I departed the nursing home a happy camper. The rest of my day was low-key: football, reading, a catnap. "Quite nice, actually," I wrote. "I am content."

If I needed reminding why Florida in winter suits me, it came with a shovel-able snow in early December. In true Rhode Island fashion, a few days later there was rain that turned to snow that turned to sleet. Messy enough to cause me to cancel what was to have been my last therapy session of the year. I wasn't happy about that, but I allowed the day to unfold and accepted it with grace. I would see Beverly in April, and we would move forward from there. It helped that I was at peace with my Christmas plans, which would have me alone except for the noon meal with ME. I was touched that my friend Linda had invited me to Christmas Eve dinner with her and Len, but for a number of reasons I chose an evening alone. I did agree to stop in at Sandra and Roberta's for coffee on Christmas morning.

Before all that, there was the annual holiday party at the nursing home. Feeling sentimental, I wore ME's special Christmas sweater (at least 25 years old and now too big for both of us). Two hours of the Elvis impersonator was a bit much for me, but watching ME sort of keep time with her hands made me smile. I missed my PondView "family," but there was no denying that I left that party with a modicum of holiday spirit. A couple days later Mike, Caryl and their oldest daughter visited ME and me in the late afternoon. I would be with them again for a night on my way to Virginia.

Christmas morning at home was quiet, bittersweet — exactly what I had expected. I think. I didn't write about the day, which says to me that there was nothing that needed telling. I found an email exchange with Sandra, which said I got to the nursing home about 11 and lunch didn't finish until about 1:30. She had written to say their plans had changed and asked if I wanted to join them for their 5:30 dinner reservation. I declined, again content to be home. I wasn't heading south for a couple days, so leaving ME after lunch would have been my usual "I love you. See you later, alligator," no doubt with "Merry Christmas" added.

Two days later, right on the schedule I had set for myself, I dropped by the nursing home. My car was packed because I planned to leave directly from there for Connecticut. This leave-taking, like the one the year before, forced me to confront the possibility that it could be the last time I saw ME. This leave-taking was different, however, because I was different. My long hello and her long goodbye were on separate tracks. Her disease was in charge of her life. I was in charge of my life — thanks to the many gifts I believe her disease has given me.

". . . If we look at this [Tarot deck Death] card the way a child looks at death, it means change — and change can offer a time of positive transformation."

Topped Chef: A Key West Food Critic Mystery
Lucy Burdette

CHAPTER 13

Unexpected Gifts

Pinpointing when I first connected positive changes in me to ME's dementia proved impossible. There seems to have been no "aha moment" but rather, typical of how I think, rumination and reflection eventually followed by resolution. My notes and emails confirmed that after ME went to memory care and then the nursing home, I periodically described an interaction with her as a gift. I also began to think about aspects of my personal growth that I described as gifts from ME's dementia. I vaguely recollect being surprised by this, puzzled to think I could see anything positive about ME's dreadful disease, concerned that others would think me daft.

As I started work on this chapter, I second-guessed my use of the word gift. When I turned to a dictionary for help, I realized why. Generally speaking, a gift is "freely given" from one person to another. Neither ME nor her disease could give me a gift. Nonetheless, when I thought about one of my important steps forward — one I was unlikely to have taken were it not for our dementia journey — it felt like a gift. So I have stuck with the word.

To organize my thoughts, I made a conscious effort to identify as many such gifts as I could. The first record I found of that was in a September 18, 2019, morning note. In a way, it was reassuring to see how long into the journey it took me to identify these gifts, to know that I had not arrived there flippantly. I was reminded of something I once read, about how we each must discover what gets us through adversity, and in that process we also might discover something meaningful about ourself.

As I made my initial list, it became clear that although it was late in the journey when I identified some gifts, others actually had come much earlier. All helped me navigate the journey. Many brought me joy. All have made possible the at-times-crazy-life I have been living since October 2013. Resilience long has fascinated me. Why is it certain individuals can recover from adversity and others cannot? How is it I came to find meaning in the pain of watching dementia disappear my partner? I don't know. But perhaps in writing about my gifts, others might see a space where they can identify their own. And in doing so, find ways to live their own best lives.

I do not rank my gifts by their "importance," not the least because many are interrelated. But without a doubt, it is fitting to begin with **Weight Watchers** (name changed to WW in September 2018). I do so not because it led me to lose 60+ pounds, which helped me get healthy, but because it brought me to the habits of mindfulness and gratitude. I also do so because even today I — so averse to groups — am incredulous about my membership and how it continues to help me.

Mindfulness and gratitude are lifelines available to any caregiver, I think, and incorporating them into one's life can never come too late. WW taught me about mindful eating from Day 1, and it wasn't long before I found myself applying it to other parts of my life. For me, mindful eating meant paying attention to what I wanted to eat and why before making conscious decisions about food choices. It played out this way, for example. One afternoon I was heading to get a snack when I stopped and said aloud, "I am not hungry, I am bored. And that is no reason to eat." And I did not. Another example: If I wanted a snack, I would ask myself, "Are you hungry enough to enjoy an apple?" If the answer was yes, I would eat an apple. Finally, when I chose to eat something not WW friendly — Key lime pie, for example — I would enjoy every bite, own the decision, and move on.

Translating mindfulness to other parts of my life remains a work in progress. Being able to concentrate on the present moment still is not always easy for me. But what has changed is my awareness about the need to do so, the calmness I can find when I do. My "allow the day to unfold, and accept it with grace" mantra is probably the most important way I practice mindfulness. It has, for example, allowed me to adjust my day's plan (something I used to resist). It helps me know when I need a break from the nursing home. It jerks me back to the present when I have allowed myself too much ruminating about the past or future.

In an early WW workshop, an 80-something woman mentioned how every morning she wrote down at least three things she was grateful for, and had been doing so for decades. WW had taught her that we feel better about ourselves when we express thanks for what we have. When we are happier, we make healthier choices. It is not helpful, for example, to feel bad about the donut(s) you ate; it is helpful to be grateful for the friend who later walked with you. And taking time to write it, or say it, is powerful. Put another way, rather than getting stuck on what has gone wrong, it is more valuable to focus on what is going well. The reset button allows us to view our setbacks as opportunities for growth.

I am reminded about how, in the midst of direct caregiving and especially in the last turbulent months, I was thankful for early morning time to myself. It was some time after joining WW that I began my morning ritual of standing at a window in the den to express my gratitude. Speaking out loud made it real for me. It continues to do so. When I finally turned caregiving over to others, I regularly expressed gratitude for those who do what I was not able to. I continue to do so. I also am regularly reminded to appreciate the "little" things in my life, such as birds singing, a cloud formation, a kind gesture, a lovely flower.

Expressing gratitude in this way also allows me to focus, if only for a moment or two, on myself. *I am thankful for* . . . . Is anything more vital for a caregiver struggling to hang on to a bit of herself? That was me for a long time. Now that focus carries into my day, reminds me that it is *my* day and I have a responsibility to myself to make the most of it.

Reuniting with my therapist is so central to my transformation from caregiver to a woman able to discover and live her best life that I write about it second only because it came two weeks after my first WW meeting. Without ME's dementia, I likely would not have returned to therapy. I would have continued meandering along the life path I was on, one that in retrospect was less fulfilling, less authentic, more closed than open.

How fortunate I felt that Beverly was still in practice, that she welcomed me back with a reassuring hug after so many years. Originally she had helped me find my way through the morass and repercussions of my long-hidden abuse. In my dedication to ME's and my book, I cited her "immeasurable wisdom [that] helped me find my way and my voice."

When finally I acknowledged how much I was in need of help to survive ME's dementia, she again offered me a way and a voice. It is because of our work that I have been able to make all the difficult decisions embedded in caregiving and guardianship. It is because of our work that, when I was ready, I was able to move beyond caregiving. It is because of our work that personal growth followed. She has helped me recognize it, has supported me during the starts and stops. To the extent I am the well-adjusted partner of someone with dementia — and I believe beyond all doubt that I am — it is because I had Beverly listening to me, guiding me in a way that allowed my truths to emerge.

Personal growth — This gift encompasses so many other gifts. Its numerous aspects, as I identify them, are works in progress. Recognizing its various pieces is a way of reflecting on my life Before Diagnosis and finding perspective on my life After Diagnosis. It is a way to examine what happened to me when I became a caregiver. It is a way to find positives amid all the pain. I include these:

I learned to ask for what I need. I am independent, strong-willed, opinionated, stoic. For a very long time, Paul Simon's song spoke to me: "I am a rock, / I am an island. / I've built walls . . . . That none may penetrate. . . . I have my books / And my poetry to protect me . . . . a rock feels no pain; / and an island never cries." Time and experiences diminished those feelings, but I continued to have trouble asking for help. I got somewhat better at it when I battled severe Lyme disease at the same time ME was caring for her mother. Once recovered, though, I went back to being me. A couple decades later, ME's illness changed that. My really big ask, of course, was getting outside help with caregiving. Since then, asking has been easier. But I must constantly work at not regressing.

I have a deeper understanding of true friendship. As Doc Ford, one of my favorite fictional characters, says in Randy Wayne White's *Everglades*: "Friendship comes with responsibilities — reliability during crisis being among them." ME and I were alike in regard to friends; we each identified a few very close, long-standing friends and many acquaintances. The same was true for us as a couple. As her illness progressed, our acquaintances fell away, as did most of her friends. My friendships, by and large, were strengthened as I shared my feelings more freely than at any point in my life. I found a depth of support — in person and long-distance — I never imagined. As the healthy half of a couple on the dementia journey, I have a life-affirming support system in my family and friends. It would be easy to concentrate on how our world shrinks during caregiving, but I think it is healthier to remember those who continue to stand with us.

I learned that I have the capacity to care beyond ME. I have known that I feel emotions deeply, but I seldom showed that — and generally only in private. Not so much anymore. Examples of how I learned to be emotionally available to others are scattered throughout the previous chapters. I am not proud of my early fears of even being inside WV and SKNRC, but I am immensely proud of overcoming those fears. Proud that I can empathize and connect with many of those who share ME's circumstance — and mine.

I made peace with others' guilt. More than once I have been told, "You must feel guilty" about moving ME out of her home. I found it difficult to respond, because I don't believe in guilt; I don't think it is a useful emotion. (Perhaps that stems from my journalism background. In the news business, we deal with decision-making based on the best information we have at a point in time. Then we go forward but continually reassess.) When my friend Luise asked me how I planned to address the question of guilt in this book, I fumbled for an answer. On reflection, that is what led me to think about second-guessing/reevaluating. Of course caregiving results in LOTS of second guessing. But it doesn't have to translate to guilt. Perhaps if, as I did, we early on came across the sentence, "Are you ready for fecal incontinence?" it would be easier. Perhaps if we learned early on that our decisions must be reduced to "Is my loved one safe and well cared for?" it would be easier. When we are honest with our answers, the path forward is clearer. That does not mean easy. That does not mean comfortable. It *does*, however, mean we are making the correct decision.

I learned to not sweat the "small stuff." For the longest time, laundry, missing clothes, finding ME without her glasses, etc. drove me crazy. My nursing-home visit would get off to a cranky start, or would end on a rocky note. I felt like a nag, and I didn't like it, but I believed I was fulfilling my responsibility to look out for ME. As I thought about that, I realized that such aggravations predated the nursing home. Much of my upset AD (and no doubt BD, too) was about the inconsequential. I know now that I felt out of control, and who enjoys that?

Focusing on something like how a household task wasn't being done "my way" — so just let me do it myself — allowed me to feel in control. I could manage my early nervousness about the nursing home by focusing on something not up to my standards. Then, at some point it dawned on me that such things did not matter. It mattered that ME was safe and cared for. It mattered that I make my time with ME as "good" as it could be. It mattered that I was prepared to advocate on her behalf if and when the situation warranted. Eventually, I also found less and less "small stuff" in my own life to get upset about. My common refrain has become, "I'm already dealing with my partner's dementia, so how bad can this (fill in the blank) be?"

I learned to find joy in "little things." As I learned to let go of minor aggravations, I also learned to appreciate things I might have overlooked in the past. I complimented ME when she was particularly well-dressed. I noticed when she had allowed an aide to polish her nails. I learned to smile at an appropriate response, like the morning I made a quick visit and when I said "good morning," she responded "good morning." And then the nurse told me she had the same thing happen earlier. Or like a spur-of-the-moment visit from Mike and Caryl, when ME wasn't sleepy. Smiled. "Talked." And when I said "You look pretty today," she said "Thank you." As she became less and less verbal, my day could be brightened by the roll of her eyes at something silly I said. I realized she was still communicating, and I learned to "read" her. This kind of joy has translated into my own life on a daily basis. I have learned that life is indeed a lot more fun — and rewarding — when we recognize the joy around us.

I learned to open myself to possibility. Early in adulthood, I was restless. I defined home as "wherever it is I am living." When I told friends I did not feel brave or adventurous, they would remind me how I willingly left jobs I liked and moved to places where I knew no one. By middle age, I had grown into a creature of habit. I liked being comfortable, knowing what I was getting into. How else to explain vacationing year after year at the same time, in the same place, even the same room or villa or house? My "comfort zone," my sister liked to remind me, was limited.

As ME's disease progressed, caregiving felt way outside my comfort zone, so I found comfort in places and activities that were familiar. As I emerged from that caregiver role, determined to figure out how I wanted to live the rest of my life, I vowed to be more open minded. I know I have succeeded. I eat differently. (I still say no to beets, however. And Brussel sprouts. And sushi.) I have attended my first ballet. I saw "Hamilton" by myself, not because I planned it that way but because that is how it worked out. I watch television differently. I listen to different music. I have said "yes" to all manner of "adventures" — some with friends, some alone. I plan, but I can also be spontaneous. I do indeed say "yes" more often than "no."

I learned to accept, not expect. One of ME's friends always asks, "Do you think she still knows you?" And for the longest time, I feared the day when she would not. That was especially true when I traveled, and was my big worry when I went to Florida for the first time. But about a month before I left for my second winter away, it struck me how unimportant that question is. It makes it all about me (or the someone not visiting because "she won't know me anyway"). I remember the activities director telling me, "They always remember the people they love." There is comfort in that. There is even more comfort in realizing that what is important is that I/we remember her.

ME is there, body and mind diminished and diminishing as the disease progresses, for sure. But her essence, her spirit — hidden from us as they may be — remain. Emerging every now and then to remind us. Such as when she tenderly patted the arm of another PondView resident, or when she responds to me with an "I love you, too." Of course the day is likely to come when she cannot respond. Of course that will be painful. But it will be a lot less so because I accepted the gift of her spirit whenever and however and for however long it emerged — and at all the other times was able to just accept being with her. The importance of accepting a loved one with dementia on her terms is vital, I believe. It's not easy, but it allows us to treasure time together. It puts the focus where it belongs: on our loved one, not on us.

The other gifts I have identified, in no particular order, are these:

The Y and exercise — When I put my mind to it, I learned, I *can* exercise regularly. I *do* make the time. And I feel good about it. In January 2016, I needed physical therapy for hip-area pain that stopped me from walking for exercise. The therapist said water aerobics or a recumbent bike would supplement therapy and my stretching routine, and she suggested I look into the Y. I wasn't interested in the aerobics (a group activity), but the Y had a number of bikes, so I joined on February 2. I remember my first ride; I think I made ten minutes at the lowest resistance and slowest speed. I persevered. I found virtual races online at Yes.Fit and signed up for one. I figured the fact I paid to record my miles would offer motivation and accountability. (WW had showed me accountability works well for me.) I was right. By the end of 2019, I had medals from 30 races and had racked up more than 3,000 miles.

Gardening at SKNRC — Late in the summer near the end of ME's first year at the nursing home, I wheeled her to the courtyard behind PondView for a bit of sunshine. The administrator and another staff member were out there, and I overheard them talking about needing to spruce things up for a photo shoot. They were looking at spots for plants, and the staff member said she would do her best, but didn't know how much time she would have. The next thing I knew, I was volunteering to help. I love to garden, I said, and had time in the next day or two to plant whatever they wanted. The staff member introduced herself; she was Dorothy, the director of environmental services. I said I would be by in the morning.

I cannot overstate the power of that chance encounter. The me who once was unnerved by the thought of walking in the front door had become the me who was comfortable enough, brave enough, to pipe up, "Let me help." It is fair to say that I never dreamed what that day would lead to, that I later would tell Beverly how I saw gardening there as our gift — mine and ME's — to the nursing home. "I want to provide smiles long after our ties to the place are gone," I explained.

That first time, I planted what Dorothy had purchased. I weeded around a few bushes and a spot with a small statue I imagined had come from a deceased resident's family. I suggested to Dorothy that if she wanted, I had perennials at home that needed dividing, and I would be glad to bring some over. I could enlarge the space around the statute to plant them. I also asked about digging out a new spot or two. I got the green light and worked into the fall. I bought bulbs for home, then ended up planting most of them there. I learned that Dorothy and I shared Midwestern roots. After several chats, I began to think of her as a friend.

The gardening was more than an outlet for my extra perennials; it was an outlet for my energy. I wasn't much interested in tending to my gardens at home, but I loved creating those at the nursing home. The following spring (2019), into the summer and through the fall, I gardened there at least once a week. Tools and supplies from home in hand, I would cheerfully work my way down the hallways, through PondView and into the courtyard. I got sweaty and dirty and loved every minute of it. Gardening — in particular perennials and fall bulbs — is an act of hope. Ever the optimist, I hoped that I would be back in 2020 to see my handiwork bloom because I would still be visiting ME.

Golf — This gift is not as easy to explain as some of the others. I have played golf on and off since I was 16, so the gift is not the game, but rather how the game has had impacts on my life during this journey. I had started playing again because ME gave me clubs one birthday. In the '90s we played often, judging from the scorecards I unearthed during my clean outs. When ME stopped playing, I did not. After I retired, thanks to my friend Libby I was able to join the Jamestown Ladies League. Those Tuesday mornings offered a welcomed dose of fellowship along with the golf. I cannot know for certain, but if I had not needed someone to stay with ME so I could golf in 2016 I don't know when I might have sought caregiving help. That was such an important step for me. I had put myself first. I was taking care of me.

The cleanup projects — The long goodbye of dementia led me to tackling tasks that often wait until after a loved one's death. Cleaning out our study, closets and basement led me on more than one occasion to curse ME for being such a packrat. (Only later did I discover I was one, too, just better organized.) But the gift was that sorting through her piles allowed me a window on her life before me. It reinforced what I knew, reminded me of things forgotten, taught me new things about her. That gift was enhanced because I did not rush through the memories, did not run from them. I found myself awash in tangible reminders of ME's professional accomplishments, how students admired her, how colleagues respected her. I was saddened by reminders of her brilliance (So many people have said of her dementia, "The worst part is she was so smart!") and angered by the disease that robbed her of that. I was comforted by the many touchstones of the life we built and the love we shared.

Early mornings — It took me until recently to finally, I hope, stop obsessing over my sleeping patterns. After reading years of notes, with way too many of them starting with a comment about my early rising, I thought "Enough!" Even as I complained, however, I recognized the importance of quiet time for myself. As ME's dementia progressed, and before I had help, early morning usually was the *only* part of the day that was all mine. I treasured it then (resented it when ME woke earlier than usual) and I treasure it now.

For one thing, this gift carved out reading time for me. Always a voracious reader, in retirement I was — surprisingly — less focused on books than at any time in my life. I meandered through them, sometimes with gaps of days between pages. Once I found myself routinely wide awake by 5 (often earlier), I began to devour books again. Nonfiction engaged my intellect and fiction spirited me away. In both, I often found wisdom, as the many passages I recorded (some used in this book) attest to. It was also in the early morning when I began to write my notes, recording events and processing what I was experiencing and, importantly, feeling.

Nick's Voxes — I remain unusually close to my three nephews, now men with families of their own, which they lovingly share. Each has supported me and ME through this journey. I single out the middle one, a teacher like me and an even more avid reader than I, for a promise he made and kept. Nick and his wife were teaching at an international school in Kazakhstan at the time of ME's diagnosis. We communicated via the walkie-talkie app Voxer. After I moved ME to memory care (by this time they were teaching in Peru), Nick told me he planned to try to Vox daily. I was touched by the gesture, and our regular "conversations" bolstered my spirits, especially on the many days his was the only human voice I heard. We talked books, sports, politics now and then. We talked about writing and about teaching. We talked about mundane moments in our days. His quirky observations and sense of humor made me laugh. I felt free to share my bad days, my frustrations. We forged a special relationship, a gift I treasure.

Florida — My being able to spend the winter in Florida was possible because of ME's dementia. And because I have been able to accept that it is OK for me to be away. Indeed, I see Florida as "proof" that I am taking care of myself. I am mentally and physically stronger in the sunshine and warmth than I am in the gray, cold and snow. I have known this for a long time, but I am certain that ME never would have agreed to "snowbirding." I am equally certain that we never would have agreed to spend winters — or some piece of them — apart. It took me months after she went to the nursing home to realize that being away does not mean running away. (I chose Florida over southern Arizona in large part because if necessary I could get home more easily.) Being away does not mean I love her less. Instead, I think it shows I love myself as much as her, and when I take care of me, I am better able to care of ME.

The nursing home — I have said often, including to a variety of staff members, that we did not choose SKNRC, it was chosen for us. And it has proved to be a good place for ME. And me. The bumps along the way are inconsequential compared to my overall satisfaction with ME's care. I need to believe that were it not so, she would be elsewhere. I am thankful that I have not had to face that. I am thankful beyond measure for the wonderful professionals for whom caring for ME is more than a job.

In a note I wrote the day before Thanksgiving 2019, I revisited 2013 — the year of ME's diagnosis — and concluded: "That was then, this is now. I am a new version of me. Maybe we should see ourselves like software updates. BFL v.??? I will have to work at filling in my numbers. . . . I am not sad about my life at this moment in time. Nor am I resigned to it. I believe I have reached an understanding of it. And in the silence of this early morning, I am ready not only for what today holds, but tomorrow and tomorrow and tomorrow. . . . I hope that in living my best life I honor all that the world — and ME — has given me."

"*People manage to rebound from great devastation; we read about them every day. . . . And then sometimes we become one of those people and are amazed, not only by our own strength but by that indomitable ability to slog through adversity, which looks like strength from the outside and just feels like every day when it's happening to you.*"

Lots of Candles, Plenty of Cake
Anna Quindlen's memoir

Epilogue

My 2020 Florida writer's retreat involved more writing and more retreating than I ever could have imagined. The story of why further illuminates just how significant dementia's unexpected gifts were and how they enabled me to continue to live my best life even during a global pandemic.

Very early on the morning of March 5, I drove my sister and brother-in-law to Southwest Florida International Airport. It was the first leg of their journey to Lima, Peru, for a two-week visit with their 7-month-old grandson. The next morning, I returned to the Fort Myers area for lunch with friends who had flown in from Philadelphia for a week's vacation. That lunch turned out to be my last social interaction for almost three months.

When Kris and Fred left for Peru, the coronavirus had been a blip on our radar screen since the first U.S. case was confirmed on January 21. With curiosity more than concern, we followed developments as they were reported in the news. By early March, however, I was admittedly anxious about them traveling, but the decision was theirs. My sister would not be deterred.

In a now-rare morning note, written the Sunday after they left, I observed that "the coronavirus has cast a pall over things. I am trying to be smart, not over-watch news, not change activity plans but remain prepared to do so if it feels wisest. I do worry about ME being in the nursing home, but I must trust in the staff there. That is all I can do." I had tickets for two baseball games and a concert, but already I was telling friends, "I don't have to go if it doesn't feel right."

Shortly, the world – and I — was caught up in the maelstrom of head-spinning change. The nursing home called on the 9th to say that visiting hours were now limited and a quick health screening would be required. On the 11th – the date the World Health Organization declared the outbreak a global pandemic – they called again to say that visitors would be prohibited effective on the 13th. More ominous, on that Friday the president declared a national state of emergency. "I am not usually alarmed by these things," I emailed my friend Luise, "but I have read the science and lots of informative journalism and am reacting accordingly." Then I quipped, "Of course isolating is not unlike my usual life."

For me, although I did not know it then, there already had been a string of lasts: last hugs, last visit to Planet Fitness, last round of golf (with handshakes!), last pizza at Bella Napoli, last bookstore trip, last grocery shopping at Publix (including extra toilet paper, at Kris' request; she had heard about shortages, I had not). There also began a steady stream of texts and emails between me and Kris. She was puzzled by the run on TP and suggested, "I still think they are over blowing the whole [coronavirus] thing considering the number of people actually infected." She optimistically hoped United Airlines would have a sale that would offer cheap tickets for our planned trip to Japan in November. "I think my plan is to book our flight before 3/31 as United is waiving all change fees on any flights booked before then," she wrote. "Seems too good of a deal not to take advantage of." I reluctantly agreed, "as long as canceling is possible."

On the 16th, Peru was locked down for two weeks. That threw a monkey wrench into their return and our March 30 departure from Florida. We discussed our options at length after it became clear they would be required to self-quarantine for 14 days once back in the States. Eventually we decided they would not return to Punta Gorda and I would drive home with all they had left behind.

At the same time, the situation in the Northeast got dicier each day. Ordinarily, a 1,400-mile solo drive would not frighten me. It would be daunting, but I would take as many days (and hotel nights) as I needed. As stay-at-home orders multiplied and shutdowns were ordered, however, that kind of travel did not feel safe. Luckily, I would be able to extend my condo stay if need be. I wrote Kris that it was "a tad unsettling being alone and knowing no one. But I think it's the best place for me right now. Caryl agrees. So did the nurse [I spoke with when I called to check on ME]. I am staying away from the pool. Lanai is great; reading out there now. Actually so HOT that being in sun [at the pool] wouldn't be fun. No problem dealing with your stuff. Playing it by ear about when I leave."

That morning I also wrote about my anxieties, and I copied something I read from AnxietyUK, about using the APPLE technique for dealing with them: Acknowledge, Pause, Pull back, Let go, Explore. My note included thoughts on "using my time to write, which means reliving the dementia journey:

> And this morning, the second or third of waking way too early, with churning brain/thoughts all over the place, feels a lot like so many of those mornings. Working my way through 2016 no doubt is the culprit. Writing this 'journal' this morning, after not doing much this entire Florida stay, feels like back then. So alone and needing to work out anxiety by acknowledging it. Thank goodness — no, thanks Beverly — I have the tools to handle this.

One thought train currently chugging along in my brain is when to go. Leave early? Extend my stay? Again, wait and see. Finally, I need to record how thankful I am for Sandra's friendship. Texting. Calling. Volunteering to shop for me pre-homecoming. It is assurance that although I am on my own, I really am not. (Others are there for me, too.) Now, on with my day. It will be a challenge, but I am in a warm place, with a roof over my head, food, books, internet, a safe place to walk. And a well-working brain. I can do this. I will do this.

It was not the only time I expressed gratitude for my circumstances even as I struggled with unsettledness. Being alone was unnerving, but it also simplified isolating. Days inside provided uninterrupted blocks of time for writing. The climate provided sunshine and temperatures conducive to walking, and being able to walk relieved stress. Two mornings later, I wrote another lengthy note to cheer myself, propel myself forward:

In my early waking moments today (4ish, again) it occurred to me that my present is akin to the past I am immersed in to write my book. Maybe revisiting — at this time — the last horrible months of ME at home and the roller-coaster months that followed is not such a good idea. Yet it is having that book project that helps me get through the day in this most unusual moment in history.

So much has changed since I wrote Monday morning. . . . Here in the States, things changed continually. More restrictions, and then more. And so it continues. "Social distancing" joined our vocabulary with lightning speed.

I am not panicky. I have concluded that staying put in Florida is the right thing for now. But I do find myself reluctant to even go out to the market, which I suppose is a good thing and what is desired. The virus is in charge. I know what precautions to take, but how can I be certain not to introduce it into my environment, which feels OK because I have been isolating?

Thank goodness for the internet, text messages and phone calls. It is disconcerting to be here, knowing no one. As long as I am healthy I can manage that. But I do wish I was managing stress a bit better. Which brings me back in time. The early waking, racing brain et al remind me of that. I hope by writing this I am beginning to empty it out. I did write Beverly yesterday. Mentioned how I realized I have the tools I need to cope emotionally. My goal today is to be more mindful of my coping strategies and, if need be, put them to good use. . . . Now, it is time to get on with my day. Whatever it holds, I WILL manage.

Turned out the day held a surprise. The nursing home called to say ME had had a short seizure and was doing okay. The news shook me up, but I knew from experience that there was nothing I could do, whether I was in Rhode Island or Punta Gorda. I had learned to receive such news but not dwell on "what ifs." Instead, to cope with my lingering anxiety about grocery shopping, I inventoried my provisions and told Kris that "I feel settled for a while, with no need to go to a store." I was still thinking I might leave at the end of March, and while I didn't want to run too low, I also didn't want to have a lot to throw out when I left. I tried not to have a departure date in mind. What I did know was that I wanted "to feel a measure of confidence on the road and in hotels, because I am working hard here to do it right." I bluntly told my friend Sandra, "I don't want to do all this and then get back, get sick and die."

My morning notes, frequent again, mixed pensiveness with anxiety with resolve, not unlike this one from March 21, a Saturday:

I just put down my book and looked up and out the open door to the lanai to see a sliver of moon just above the tree line. Its light, light orange tint is unlike mornings past, when I caught it higher in the sky. Somewhere nearby, songbirds have awakened. They don't realize, do they, how different the world is? It seems to have taken only an instant, though it really is a work in progress. Result unknown. Territory uncharted.

I am not unhappy to be awake early . . . because this new day is a gift, one I hope to take full advantage of. When I greeted the world in my usual fashion, one thing I mentioned being grateful for was that so far in my "isolating" I have not said, "I am bored." I also said I am grateful to have tools to deal with my anxieties and emotions, even if it takes those tools awhile to kick in. Which happened in my ruminating minutes of semi-wakefulness. When I realized that I do not have to talk myself down from a mountain of concerns/worry/anxiety, but rather just have to talk myself back from the edge. And so I did.

Thus here I sit, marveling at the wonder of another dawn and the promise of sunshine and heat. I cannot know what the day will bring. There is so much I cannot control. But I can try to live my best life again today. And that is a gift.

By late March, I had settled into a generally comfortable routine. "Good thing I am low maintenance," I wrote Luise. I overheard a neighbor mention ordering groceries online from Walmart, which offered contact-free pickup. I checked it out and happily signed on. I had socks that worked well as "gloves" and a doctor on YouTube who taught me how to wipe down my purchases. I had vowed to walk mornings and evenings, and I did. That meant I had to get dressed, and for the most part I stayed dressed until after dinner. I made healthy meals and ate lunch and dinner at the table. I worked on my book for a couple hours in the morning and again after a leisurely lunch break that included relaxing and reading on the lanai. I discovered Pandora and was elated to create stations of music by artists I had not thought about in years. I lost access to CBS but made do with a bit of local news and the national news on NBC. Friday night was movie night. Weekends were for changing things up. I spread out my few chores across the week. I monitored developments in Rhode Island and quickly judged that our governor was doing a bang-up job of managing things. I thought the opposite of Florida's leadership, and the president was the source of pessimism and despair. Making a slight adjustment, I returned to the mantra that got me through dementia days: Allow the day to unfold, and deal with it!

As March drew to a close, I was pleased to learn during the quarterly care-plan meeting for ME that the nursing home remained free of the coronavirus. (Imagining how busy the staff must be, I resisted the urge to check in too often.) I was elated to get a photo of ME (needing a haircut, like the rest of us); my heart smiled for days. I was encouraged by my ability to sort out my feelings (and solve writing problems) during my evening walks. To keep myself from dwelling on coronavirus concerns, I began answering questions for myself, such as: What are five things you saw today? What are five things you felt today? What are five things you enjoyed today? Name something you did today that was new for you. What is your agenda for tomorrow? I was, I realized, expanding the gifts of mindfulness and gratitude that I received from ME's illness.

On one of those walks, I named three habits (I labeled them My 3 Rs) that were getting in my way. Clearly they were exacerbated by isolating during the current crisis, but I knew I had owned them for some time. They were: Rehash, Rehearse, Ruminate. I explored them in a morning note: "I rehash incidents, conversations, decisions, whatever. There is little value in doing this, other than to stir up anxieties. I rehearse so many things, be it a social media post, an email, a text, a point I want to make, and more. Again, the value in this is similar to above. Ruminate is a word I have used a lot since ME's illness, and until a few days ago it was my go-to descriptor. I now see it as extreme rehashing, with more judgment."

I vowed to work at reducing how often I did those things. From that point on, as I caught the behavior I told myself, STOP. "I don't want to jinx myself," I wrote, "but it seems to be helping. The three nights since, I have slept better than in ages. Indeed, I have declared the bed to be a Rehash/Rehearse Free Zone! The power was in naming the behaviors, which has allowed me to work on them!!!"

And then it was April. I was supposed to be in Rhode Island. I was supposed to be bounding into the nursing home, smiling broadly and ready to hug ME. Instead, I remained in Punta Gorda, my future one of questions, not answers. If March had required me to regularly tamp down anxiety, April required me to remain patient as events continued to unfold at an unfamiliar pace. I discovered that the unpredictable, ever changing dementia journey with ME had prepared me well.

The question that family and friends invariably asked in every phone conversation, text exchange, FaceTime call or Zoom session was, "When are you leaving?" By April, my stock answer had become, "When it feels right, and I hope that is in a couple of weeks." But of course, the "right time" was a moving target. I continued to take aim, then would lose confidence, then would confront information that had me reconsidering yet again. For example, at the beginning of April I was comfortable with a plan to stay in Florida until at least the middle of the month. I got groceries for two more weeks. Then my friends Libby and John returned to Rhode Island from Hilton Head, and after she described their "uneventful" trip I immediately began contemplating packing my car and leaving in a few days. I wrote about my internal struggle this way:

> Immediately after hanging up my brain whirls. Maybe I should go soon. But I have all this food. But is that reason enough to stay? I read about Georgia, where there is a stay-home order but it does not seem to include hotels. I could be ready to go as early as Monday.

> I drive myself a little wacky. I cannot seem to drop it. Through dinner. On my walk. Wishing, oh wishing, I did not have to make this decision alone. I do manage some TV viewing, finally, and with it a bit of peace. Thankfully I fall asleep when I go to bed. But awake about 2:30. Ruminating. Back to sleep. Awake about 4:30, finally up about 5:15. New book finally hooks me. But I also know I have to write in order to work this out:

> My goal remains to feel/be safe.

> *I feel safe in this cocoon I have created here.*

> *I will feel safe in my car, another cocoon.*

> *I will feel safe in my house, once I am there.*

> So what I am uneasy about is those points in traveling from here to there where I am likely to have some interaction with other people. Will I be less uneasy about that in a week or 10 days or whenever?

Probably not.

Is my uneasiness unreasonable?

I don't think so. And besides, it is what I feel. I think of [the fictional] Doc Ford's line that fear is not a thing, it is a warning!

Can I take steps for my travel that could help me feel less uneasy? Yes.

I can — go with my plan to monitor the week ahead, reassess, then decide.

I can — make my mask.

I can — organize my travel techniques, make a list, prepare methodically — in other words, use this week to get ready.

I can — acknowledge there is no way to be 100% safe, so I will be nervous, but that cannot prevent me from going home — which is where I am ready to be!!!

Whew . . . I think this helps.

For the first time, I framed my situation this way: "My responsibility to myself is the same as my responsibility to ME, which is to do my best to ensure I am safe and well cared for. That is what has governed my decision-making to this point. I am here, and will stay here as long as need be." Late in the afternoon, after an hourlong conversation with Kris, I was resolute about staying put, as they had decided to do in Peru. Afterward, I texted her, "Thanks again for being my wise sister. I've got this now."

A couple days later, I told my friend Linda that "I have quit thinking about when I will leave, and that helps. . . . Life in Rhode Island would not be any different than here, for the most part. And here I am able to walk outdoors and be on the lanai for as much fresh air as I want." It helped that a few days before, when I had seen the guy from next door working on his car, I uncharacteristically introduced myself. We chatted. I explained my situation and learned of theirs. At least I now had their names, and they mine. That felt like something good.

It would be a stretch to describe myself as content over the following couple of weeks, yet my days in isolation were generally drama-free. The gift of "accept, don't expect" was as applicable to my cocoon as it was to my visits with ME. As much as I wanted to support a Punta Gorda bookstore, I was more comfortable buying for my Kindle. I tried a virtual WW meeting. I won the Earth Day raffle I had entered to support a business back home. I got my "stimulus" check and put it to work doing good back home. I was impressed by the community support there, and thought about ways I might feel more comfortable if I were in Rhode Island.

Easter almost caught me by surprise; indeed, I had not bought anything for a holiday meal when I picked up my Walmart order a few days before. In a long email to Linda, I wrote of a low-key day:

> I had no eggs to dye, so I made my masks. A sharper scissors would have helped. Long FaceTime last evening with nephew and family in Japan, then this morning with the Virginia crew. So that made the day special. About to sauté a couple of chicken thighs and cook pasta. Did another two-week Walmart pickup Wednesday morning. Maybe that will be my last. Yes, HOT for at least next five days. Luckily there was a bit of breeze for my 7:45 a.m. walk, and hoping for same after dinner. It won't be nearly as tasty as your cake, but I have a chocolate mug cake to look forward to. Finally, HBO has made a bunch of movies available for free viewing on Roku. I watched "Nancy Drew and the Hidden Staircase" earlier, now watching something called

"Blinded by the Light." A strange life I am living at the moment.

Strange indeed. I eventually used up my postcard stash (and Kris'), so my weekly correspondence to ME required creativity. Fortunately, I had brought my coloring books and pencils. I found the least complex picture, colored it over a few days, and wrote a letter on the back (always ending, "See you later alligator). I finally ordered a notebook with groceries. Then I could print on the lined paper and, like a kid, draw a simple flower for decoration. Coloring distracted me when I tired of writing or reading, and on one level I hoped my art amused ME – or at least the aide who read to her.

When Governor Raimondo extended Rhode Island's stay-at-home order until mid-May, I focused on a departure timed to then. On April 17, I took a "baby step" outside my cocoon, which up to then I had left only to go to Walmart or make a weekly drive at highway speed for the sake of my car. I ordered take-out, with contact-free pickup, from a favorite restaurant. Driving there was eerie. I thought about how Kris and I had been on some of those streets every day, and how I had not gone that way in five weeks. It felt odd to be so proud of doing something so mundane. I savored the food, especially the Key lime pie.

A few days later I received the call I had feared. ME's nursing home had its first COVID-19 cases, which were on the locked dementia wing. I was aware of the horrifying percentages of deaths in such facilities, and was glad to know that all residents and staff were getting tested. After the call, I took a deep breath and called Mike. Then it was a matter of waiting. I was remarkably calm that evening. I knew that, as with ME's dementia, the disease was in charge and even if I were home there was nothing I could do. I was more of a wreck the next morning, however, perhaps because I realized it had been about this same time the year before that we thought ME might be dying. When I got the call on the 22nd to report that her test came back negative, I physically felt how powerful my anxiety had been when I exhaled a huge sigh of relief. I was further calmed when I learned every resident on her hallway also had tested negative, and the facility's positives were confined to the locked wing.

Going forward, the fact that the chilly and rainy spring continued at home helped me remain patient about staying put. The weather in Punta Gorda was delightful, for the most part. I marveled at seeing different birds than we saw in winter. My writing was going well. I had fallen in love with Doc Ford and was racing through Randy Wayne White's series. I was taking good care of myself with twice-daily walks and generally healthy meals. I did long for a haircut, and joked with my nephew Bill, who cut his boys' hair, that I was ready for him to give me a buzz cut.

I realized I might be ready to make the trip north after the most ordinary of decisions. It was Sunday, April 26, and when I tried to turn on the TV to stream music after lunch I discovered the remote's batteries were dead. I can do without a lot of things, I said to myself, but not the TV. So without giving myself time to fret, I slipped into flip-flops, put on my no-sew mask for the first time, walked to the Family Dollar behind our parking lot, spotted batteries immediately, paid for them and returned to my condo. My first outing lasted about 10 minutes. I felt emboldened.

Within a couple days I returned to packing Kris' belongings. I texted her that "I am officially freaking out" about being able to get everything into the car. I thought increasingly about leaving. On Friday, May 1, I mapped a route of three 500-mile driving days, identified towns with familiar hotels, called them about restrictions. I finished packing Kris' stuff and began work on mine. I also began packing the car. I texted Tom, the condo owner, to say I would be leaving soon. I studied the weather forecasts and determined that starting my trip on Sunday or Monday would work. As so often is the case, arriving at the decision was difficult, but once it was made I moved forward expeditiously and efficiently.

Saturday morning I texted my friend Sandra that I was "enjoying one last cool morning, with the lanai doors wide open. But tomorrow is the right time to leave. I can do this!" I made hotel reservations, confident that I would be as safe as possible. I finally heard from Tom, who said I was free to stay as long into May as I wanted – at no charge! I replied that it was a good thing my car was three-quarters packed or I might have been tempted. In reality, though, by then I was eager to get home. I also was anxious about making the trip, but believed I was being as smart about it as humanly possible.

My plan was to be on the road by 7:30 Sunday morning. I was. It took me much of the day to settle myself down. As expected, once I had made my way to I-95 North I felt better. From Savannah north was familiar territory, thanks to the years of visiting Hilton Head. I heard a new song, "This Too Shall Pass," written by Mike Love of the Beach Boys in response to the pandemic, and a line in it moved me forward: "Be cautious but don't be afraid." That was how I tried to approach my first foray into the larger coronavirus world.

The three-day drive, for the most part, was as easy as it could be. The route got more familiar each day, but the lightness of its traffic was anything but familiar. I used cruise control more than in my entire driving career. The air was so clear, I looked again and again at the New York City skyline as I crossed the new Cuomo bridge. And thought of all the suffering, pain, death — and heroism — in the city. The 1,425 miles flew by at 73 mph! I pulled into my driveway at 12:45 p.m. on Tuesday, May 5. I unpacked only the essentials. After friends dropped off groceries, I settled into my recliner, wrapped in my Florida quilt trying to get warm, while I exchanged texts with family.

The next morning, I started my lengthy note about the trip this way: "It feels as if I am living in an episode of 'The Twilight Zone.' Returned to a house exactly as I left it on December 27. And everything else has changed! So much to process. One day at a time. With two weeks of self-quarantine now under way, there will be plenty of time for thinking."

Re-entry was difficult and more than a bit depressing. It felt weird not to be able to visit ME. Being twelve minutes away was so much more difficult than being three days away! I allowed myself several days of funk, of no schedule, of loungewear. Lots of TV. Unmindful eating, although I did a virtual WW workshop with my Thursday gang. Numerous texts and chats. On Monday, May 11, I woke up and declared that it was time to get back to the me who managed so well in Florida. To get dressed. To tackle tasks. To have at least an inkling of a plan for what I wanted to do. "I will allow this day to unfold, and the next, and the next," I wrote. "I will be cautious, but not afraid. I will step out into this new world, that has its own schedule and is full of unknowns. And I will do my best to continue to live my best life."

What I most wanted to do was visit ME. Because I knew she was well cared for, I took it in stride that I could not. Every update from the nursing home, every retest, however, meant waiting for a phone call and hoping for the best. Negative. Negative. Negative. We FaceTimed on our 30th anniversary (May 29) and on her 79th birthday (May 30). Seeing her in real time was celebration enough.

It would be another month before I was finally allowed a no-contact visit. June 25 — two days shy of six months since I had last seen her, and one day shy of three years since I had moved her to memory care. Afterward, I sent a photo of us to family and friends, along with this message: "My heart is grinning. A plexiglass barrier can't block love! She was sleepy, but responded a couple of times. Looked about the same as December. Best 10 minutes of the last six months."

Rhode Island
July 3, 2020

"i carry your heart with me(i carry it in

My heart) i am never without it(anywhere)

I go you go, my dear; and whatever is done

By only me is your doing, my darling)

E. E. Cummings

Acknowledgements

Within the book, I offer explicit and implicit thanks to many family members, friends and others for sharing this journey. To avoid repetition — a bane of editors such as myself — I do not name them here. But I do offer each of you my heartfelt appreciation and love.

I am immensely grateful for the five wise, wonderful women who read an early draft of my book: Luise Forseth, Jane Halligan, Sue Johnpeter, Mary Ann Quince and Beverly Serabian. Your insightful comments and suggestions brought clarity to my story and made the book better. Your supportive responses gave me the courage to go forward with publication. Sorry I made each of you cry.

Sue Johnpeter, you deserve additional kudos for reading the manuscript a second time, providing feedback on the cover and helping me proof the finished book. You saved me from embarrassing errors of all sorts. Any that remain are my responsibility. Beyond that, your timing was perfect and your advice spot-on when you encouraged me to hire a professional designer.

David James, you were an absolute pleasure to work with. I am over the moon with your design. Your attention to detail surpassed mine!

Barry Petersen's "Lessons Learned" essay was life-changing for me, as I suspect it has been for many. My public thank you is necessary but not sufficient.

Caryl and Mike, thanks again for the Bluetooth keyboard/iPad case you gave me many Christmases ago. Without it, writing this book would have been so much more difficult and time-consuming.

I don't know how to sufficiently pay homage to the staff at South Kingstown Nursing and Rehabilitation Center. You are overworked, underpaid professionals who provide a safe, compassionate, loving environment for our most vulnerable seniors. You taught me much! You were my heroes long before the pandemic! I am not naming you only because it would break my heart to forget someone.

Kris Parmentier, I don't understand your devotion to *Outlander*, but I thank you for reading Book 5 in the series during our first Florida winter and sharing its last line with me. I saved it to share with ME.

ME, "When the day shall come that we do part, if my last words are not 'I love you' – ye'll ken it was because I didna have time."

Made in the USA
Monee, IL
14 July 2024

61276079R00157